Surrendered Wives
Empowered Women

Surrendered Wives
Empowered Women

Inspiring, True Stories of Real Women Who
Revitalized the Intimacy, Passion and Peace
in Their Relationships

By
Laura Doyle
and

Kathy Murray, Gladys Diaz, Shazia Ali, Mari-Jean Anderson, Norita Bonin,
Sheri Byrd, Darlene Davis, Michelle Edsall, Courtney Elder, Sarah Ellis,
Jineen Glover, Cheryl Johnson, Julie Koehn, Bonnie Mottram, Sue Prince,
Tatianna Jane Solibun, Leticia Vasquez, and Katherine Wong-Velasco

St. Monday, Inc.

ISBN: 0967305829
ISBN-13: 978-0967305820

St. Monday, Inc.
1532 Keel Drive
Newport Beach, CA 92625
http://lauradoyle.org
send feedback to Laura@lauradoyle.org

Printed in the United States of America

10   9   8   7   6   5   4   3   2   1

Editing by Megan Askew
Copyediting by Stefanie Herron
Laura Doyle author photo by Tara Shannon
Cover design by Thomas Elder
Printed by Create Space

To place orders through St. Monday Inc:
Tel: 800-466-2028
email: info@lauradoyle.org

Significant discounts for bulk sales are available. Please contact Kathy Murray
at Kathy@lauradoyle.org or 949-729-9843

To my courageous, compassionate, and dedicated Certified Coaches for your faith and support in my mission to end world divorce. I couldn't do it without you. I am eternally grateful.

Contents

Introduction

Becoming the Woman You Always Wanted to Be

Laura Doyle
Founder, Laura Doyle Connect

Some people find the phrase "Surrendered Wife" shocking and offensive. They think it means "obedient wife" or "subservient wife." When paired with the phrase "Empowered Woman," it can be even more upsetting because these phrases seem mutually exclusive.

A Surrendered Wife is an empowered woman because she lets go of trying to control the things she can't, like the weather, heavy traffic, and other people, including her husband. That leaves her with more energy for the things she can control, like herself.

A Surrendered Wife knows she can't change anyone but herself. She won't try to change her husband by telling him what to eat, what to wear, or what to do at work. Instead, she focuses on her own happiness and that, in turn, fosters intimacy.

But how does surrendering give you more intimacy in your relationship? How does it make you feel more confident and connected? How does it empower you to create the kind of relationship that you know, deep down, is possible?

That's what this book is all about. This collection of true stories describes how real women have applied the skills in real marriages and single-handedly saved, healed, and transformed them.

This book chronicles the experiences of passionate women who not only learned The Six Intimacy Skills at the highest level but are also helping other women to create magical relationships. These women have been certified as Laura Doyle Relationship Coaches and work shoulder-to-shoulder with me on my mission to end world divorce.

Surrendering is a gateway to living purposefully because it requires courage. It's deciding to choose faith instead of fear.

It means becoming aware of the times you're tempted to bulldoze when all you need to say is what you want. It's about being vulnerable instead of making demands. It means expressing gratitude even if what you have isn't perfect and focusing like never before on your own desires and choices.

Surrendering means being a better receiver and a better listener. You become more respectful of men—especially your man.

When you surrender, you become more cherished by your man. You turn the clock back to the beginning of the relationship, to when you felt adored and you were crazy about him.

Surrendering is calming. It's relaxing.

Surrendering in my marriage is the best self-improvement program I've ever undertaken.

What I Know about You

One thing I know about you is that you're a seeker. You want to understand relationships. You want to feel inspired and empowered. Having a fulfilling relationship is deeply important to you.

Why else would you pick up a collection of stories from eighteen women who have transformed their relationships from unsatisfying or downright depressing to vibrant and amazing?

You want to learn from these women—to stand on their shoulders and use their experience to quickly gain insight into what they have learned. You want an insider's glimpse of the tips that have brought about the most connection and intimacy. You want access to the brain trust of the wise women who coach and train on The Six Intimacy Skills. You want inspiration and motivation to do what they did.

I think that's exciting because what you're seeking is exactly what started the most exhilarating, terrifying, and gratifying journey of my life—learning how to love and be loved in return.

It turns out that it really is all it's cracked up to be.

But previously my relationship with my husband of twenty-six years was mystifying, frustrating, and painful.

I was completely unequipped to nurture an intimate relationship when I married at the age of twenty-two. There was no Relationships 101 course at my school. My parents are divorced, and I was following their failed recipe for happily-ever-after in my own marriage—and edging ever closer to the same results.

I thought I would just *know* how to have a playful, passionate relationship, but for a long while, I didn't, and I couldn't crack the code. I read popular relationship books but saw no improvement. Years of marriage counseling made things worse. Even though (or maybe because) I followed conventional wisdom, I was stuck in the painful, lonely mud.

Those were dark years. I was doing everything wrong but didn't realize it. I believed our problems were all because of my husband, John, and that our home was filled with tension and hostility because of his rotten attitude. I was absolutely certain that I was the more spiritually evolved, smarter, and more mature person.

I Was Wrong About Absolutely Everything

I know now that I always had the key. As the wife, I'm the keeper of our relationship—the one with the feminine gifts that contribute to connection and a lifelong bond.

It turns out that I was not more spiritually evolved than my husband. I was angry, scared, and complaining most of the time. There's nothing spiritual about that.

I was not smarter; I was making a lot of extra work for both of us.

And I was not more mature; I was more like a martyr.

I have to laugh now because it seems so ridiculous looking back. What was I thinking?

I just didn't know any better. I did the best I could with what I knew.

Then I had an epiphany seventeen years ago. That's when things got a lot better for my marriage, my other relationships, my career, my confidence, and my dignity.

As I was writing this passage, my husband brought a cup of tea into my office and gave me a quick kiss. So apparently he doesn't have a rotten attitude anymore either.

One More Thing I Was Wrong About

When I was fantasizing about divorce and wondering what I'd ever seen in my husband, I never dreamed that there were so many other women who were having the same struggles.

I thought I was uniquely, incurably flawed with my urge to control and not appear vulnerable, without even understanding what vulnerability looked like.

I thought I was alone. And because of that, I was ashamed of our struggles. I wanted to appear to my family and friends as if I had a good marriage because I didn't want to lose status in my tribe.

One day, I finally admitted things were bad—really bad. That's when I discovered I wasn't alone.

As I opened up to friends in desperation, other women admitted they were struggling too. Now I see that I would never have discovered The Six Intimacy Skills at all if I hadn't finally started admitting that John and I were struggling as a couple.

The End of Life as I Knew It

When I first discovered The Six Intimacy Skills, I remember thinking that a veil had been lifted and I could finally see how I actually had power over the culture at my house. It could be loving and fun or distant and tense—it was all up to me! I walked around with my mouth open for the rest of the day in wonder at this realization.

But even once I had that knowledge, it wasn't easy to just stop being a controlling shrew. In order to jump that chasm, what I did—what I had to do—was pass on the discovery to other women.

So I quit controlling my husband and started controlling my girlfriends instead. I would say, "Here's what you should do. Apologize for being disrespectful when you said he was a slob."

For some reason, they did what I suggested. Through hearing myself apply my best thinking to their relationships, it started to sink in for me as well. That's when my marriage got magical. That's when I started to feel the butterflies in my stomach again when he looked at me a certain way. That's when I saw his face light up when I came home.

I came up with the idea to have a small support group on the topic of marriage. Five of us attended our first meeting in my living room. One had a cousin who wanted to know what we were doing, but lived on the other side of the country and couldn't attend our meetings.

I decided to write a book about what I'd learned from the long-married wives, my own experiments, and those meetings. That book was *The Surrendered Wife*, which tells the whole embarrassing story of how I went from controlling shrew to cherished, ridiculously happy wife by way of trial and error.

I self-published a meager 2,500 copies. Two years later Simon & Schuster reprinted *The Surrendered Wife*, which debuted on the *New York Times* bestseller list. It was published in sixteen languages in twenty-seven countries. It sold hundreds of thousands of copies and started a worldwide movement with a simple system for having intimacy, passion, and peace.

I had no idea what I was in for when I included my email address and phone number in the book.

An avalanche of women contacted me saying they felt I was writing about them. They wanted to know where I'd hidden the recording device to capture their conversations and reprint them in the book. Most of all, they wanted me to help them with their struggling relationships.

Of course, I couldn't help everyone, but I tried to anyway. I felt overwhelmed and inadequate.

All I could do was point everyone who asked for help to Surrendered Circles, gatherings of friends to support each other with practicing the principles of surrendering. Over the years, thousands of women have started Surrendered Circles in their living rooms.

While I included a format for such Circles in The Surrendered Wife, unfortunately there just wasn't enough structure to the Circles. The leaders didn't have training to run them, and the

Circles largely fizzled out. So Surrendered Circles weren't the answer I was hoping they would be.

The Answer to My Unspoken Wish

Thankfully, amazing women emerged to help. They called me, sent letters in the mail and emailed me. They reached out from all corners—from Malaysia and Mexico, the Netherlands and Hong Kong, the UK and all over the United States.

They were passionately committed to learning and practicing The Intimacy Skills. They needed help themselves but also wanted to know how they could show other women the secrets that were rocking their relationships and their world.

Some were right at divorce's door—separated and seeing attorneys. Others had visited numerous marriage counselors with no improvement. Still others, while not on the brink of divorce, knew that the sizzle was gone.

Each one used the skills to create a relationship that fulfilled her vision: passionate, playful, and gratifying.

Luckily for me, some women insisted that I train them to help others with The Six Intimacy Skills. If they hadn't been so determined, I would likely have retreated in my own fear. I still get dazed sometimes when I realize I'm the CEO of an international coaching organization.

But here's what kept me going and continues to motivate me everyday: Certified Laura Doyle Relationship Coaches are remarkable women like none I've met anywhere else. They have the biggest, wisest hearts. They support each other, their clients, and me with all their might. They're vulnerable and brave, and they love what they do. It's my privilege to get to work with and know them.

Each of them had a breakdown in her love life. Reading and implementing *The Surrendered Wife* remedied that, and experiencing this transformation was an irresistible clarion call to end world divorce by starting with her own.

That's one of the things we're most proud of about our coaching—that each of our coaches has experienced transformation in her own romantic life. She was lonely, struggling, or close to divorcing.

Then she had a breakthrough. She learned how to use her own influence and feminine gifts to make her relationship sweet and exciting again. Or she created a tender, lasting relationship after struggling with dating and not finding the right guy.

And her transformation is what makes her uniquely qualified to show another woman how to do the same thing. She's been down that difficult road already, and she knows what her clients need to do to get where they want to go. Experience is more critical than any certificate or diploma could ever be when it comes to guiding other women on the same path.

If We Can Do It, You Can Too

If you're looking for support implementing the Intimacy Skills to have more intimacy, passion, and peace, you'll find it in these pages. Each woman's story is full of pure gold that you can take on board your own life. If she can practice the Intimacy Skills to create a fulfilling marriage, so can you.

For even more support on how to adopt new habits that will help you feel desired, cherished, and adored every day for life, you may want to consider getting your own coach.

If you're craving immediate relief from a crisis or just some guidance on how to handle your unique situation, private relationship coaching may be just what you're looking for. You can find out more at http://lauradoyle.org/marriage-relationship-coaching/.

Our coaches have gone through rigorous testing and ongoing training. Their superpowers include being experts on The Six Intimacy Skills and the ability to transform lives through weekly or biweekly phone calls. They are the authentic relationship role models we all wish we'd had growing up.

They also have the most important qualification of all: an intimate, passionate, peaceful relationship.

And now, it's my great honor and privilege to introduce to you eighteen of these remarkable, courageous coaches who, in many ways, are just like you.

Their stories spell it all out: what was broken in their relationships, what they did differently, how it changed, and what their relationships are like now.

And I hope you get that, if I can do it—if the women whose stories follow can do it—then you can too.

Chapter 1

Safe, Secure, and Surrendered

Kathy Murray

Senior Relationship Coach, Laura Doyle Connect

I married young to escape my family home, where I wasn't physically or emotionally safe. I fell in love hard and fast, choosing a gentle, safe man to marry. I wanted more than anything to feel protected and secure so I could avoid the anxiety and distress I had endured in my childhood.

Soon into my marriage, however, I realized that I wasn't feeling so safe and protected, nor did I feel secure, because many nights my husband wouldn't come home after work. He often went to a bar or a party, leaving me alone with our two young babies. I didn't know how to stop being so angry at him for not coming home at night and helping with the kids. My insecurity, rage, and fear prevented me from understanding how to make things go back to the way they had been before we were married—when we were happy, in love, and had a lot of fun together. My husband had been attentive to my feelings back then, and I had felt safe and protected.

Now that we had kids and the responsibilities of keeping a home, I didn't feel that way anymore. I didn't know what to do, but I was desperate for a change, so I told my husband that if he didn't shape up by the end of the month, we were done! I honestly thought I could shock him into becoming the husband and father I needed and wanted him to be.

To my surprise, my husband moved out before the month was up.

I was the one who was shocked! I didn't think he would actually leave—I was just trying to get him to grow up and show up. I loved my husband; what I didn't love was what was happening in our relationship. I wanted to make him change, but I didn't know how, so I just threatened to leave and, instead, *he* left.

Our marriage soon ended in divorce, and a huge battle over child support, visitation, and custody ensued. I found myself a single parent to two young children, and I really felt like everything was entirely my husband's fault for not seeing what I had needed. My anger towards him and my belief that he was incapable of growing up resulted in our children rarely seeing their father for almost a decade. I tried to control everything not only during our marriage but during the subsequent divorce, and that control cost our children a relationship with their father for much of their early childhood. I'm deeply saddened by the lost years they could have spent together.

Even through the divorce and struggles of being a single mom, I thought I had things "under control." My home was peaceful, organized, and had predictable routines. Things were being handled my way and, even though it was hard, it felt safe and comfortable. My kids were too young to know any better or to suspect I was controlling, demanding, opinionated, and, quite frankly, scared and insecure.

They thought their dad didn't love or want them. Little did we know, he not only loved and wanted them but he painfully missed them and didn't know how to overcome his new wife's objection to seeing them. Her resistance was likely due to the fact that he had to go through me to see his children! It was a painful time, but soon my life and my children's lives would change for the better.

A year after my divorce, Doug and I met on a blind date, and right away I knew I liked him. He was handsome, mature, and caring. He made me feel beautiful and respected while still being a responsible, loving father to his own children, which I so admired. Doug and I dated for three years before he popped the question. I happily said yes, and we blended his two kids plus my two into our family of six.

I knew I wanted to do whatever I could to create the kind of relationship where I felt secure, safe, and cherished. Soon into our marriage, however, we found ourselves fighting about everything. I was afraid to let anyone know the truth, so I pretended that everything was great. I had no idea that pretending would eventually catch up with me. Friends often asked about the secret to our "marital bliss." I was embarrassed about our struggles and didn't want anyone to know I was failing in my marriage again.

Desperate to alter my reality to match my fantasy, I took classes, read books, and relentlessly sought answers. Why was I so angry with him anyway?

I've often wondered if my difficult childhood is what made it hard for me to have a loving, intimate relationship. I knew I'd been blessed to have long-lasting friendships, four wonderful children, amazing first and second husbands, not to mention a successful career. I felt fortunate that I didn't go down a road of self-destruction like many with such childhoods. I wasn't a drug addict or prostitute, but I was a rageaholic control freak!

My rage kept me from creating the intimate, passionate, and loving connection with my husband that I truly wanted. I didn't realize that questioning his every move and verbally expressing my doubt in his abilities would make him disinterested in me, but it did. I told myself I was just trying to help him, but I also knew it didn't feel good when my husband no longer held my hand or whispered sweet things in my ear.

Every day I told him what to wear and what to do, both professionally and around the house. I controlled how we spent and invested all our money. I would even refold the laundry he had folded or change the way he had set up the online banking because I didn't think he had done it right. He responded by shouting. Our home was volatile and had so much uncertainty and tension— exactly what I'd wanted to avoid because of my childhood. I was sure that if Doug would only see things my way, we could save our marriage and stop the fighting.

I was lonely, unhappy, and devastated at the thought of a second divorce, but I also felt powerless to fix things. I thought our failing marriage was entirely my husband's fault, just as I had with my first husband. I couldn't figure out why everything went to hell. I blamed his kids while he blamed mine. We'd send our eldest son away when the fights got too intense, certain it was his fault because he showed disregard for us and our rules, even dropping out of high school, but would realize that even when he was gone, we'd still fight. We blamed each other too, and soon the distance rose to unbearable heights.

Desperate to fix the situation, I decided I needed some advice on my long list of issues with my husband and his kids. I hired a therapist to help me figure out how I could get them to change. I just wanted to figure out what I could do to stop the fighting, or else I felt I was going to have to get out—again. The therapist took my money each week, scheduling more and more appointments, but nothing changed in my marriage. Eventually, it got so bad that Doug and I started sleeping in separate bedrooms and barely talked to each other, let alone made love.

One night, I was complaining about Doug to my girlfriend (again) when she shocked me by saying, "Either shut up, or get a divorce."

I was stunned she would say such a hurtful thing to me! I also knew I had to do something—I just didn't know what it was. We had gone to marriage counseling, taken transformational courses, read books, and kept up the front with our friends and extended family that "we were great!" I was already in therapy and had taken numerous personal development courses over the previous ten years, but nothing I did was changing my pattern of criticizing, correcting, and controlling my husband and our kids.

I was devastated, so I booked a flight to visit my mother. I knew I needed to chill out and take a break from the daily fights and figure out what to do. I brought books with me, hoping to find some answers. One of them was *The Surrendered Wife*. As I read, I felt like Laura was writing about me. I sobbed as I turned each page. I began to realize just how nasty I'd been to my husband and how close I was to losing him if I didn't make a change.

While reading, I felt ashamed and embarrassed for how I'd spoken to my husbands. For the first time, I realized my part in my failed first marriage and, if I didn't do something quickly, soon-to-be failed second marriage. It was very painful. I cried that night and all the next day, but I also finally felt understood. Laura understood my pain because she'd had the same pain, made the same mistakes, and still saved her marriage. Underneath all of the pain, I began to feel a glimmer of hope.

When I returned home, I decided to try something Laura suggested in her book. When Doug asked which cell phone service he should pick, I said, "Whatever you think." Those were completely foreign words to me, but I wanted to test the principles I'd read in Laura's book, so I just said what she suggested.

My husband was nervous because he was sure he would blow it and hear about it from me later, so he asked again, "No, really. What should I do?"

Again I said, "Whatever you think," but then added, "I trust you to make that decision."

This was so unlike me, and while it was uncomfortable, I was desperate to try anything to end the fights and close the distance between us.

That night we crawled into bed together for the first time in months, and my husband said, "Boy, you have been so nice tonight." Tears rolled down my cheeks as I thought to myself, "Oh my gosh! This works!" I felt like I had turned my marriage around in one night!

Next, I fired my therapist, contacted Laura, and insisted that we had to meet. She agreed, and we met at a coffeehouse near her home. Laura listened as I told her of my pain and the shortcomings in my marriage. I didn't feel judged or embarrassed; she made me feel understood and was so compassionate. She told me I could save my marriage and have the kind of intimacy and connection I craved, and she suggested I continue to practice her principles. With her encouragement, I began to believe it was possible to have the intimate, loving connection with my husband that I so desperately wanted. I was willing to do whatever it took— including telling the truth about my marriage.

Once I realized I needed to do something other than complain to my friend and a therapist, I took action to gain more tools and to become accountable, despite my childhood or other justification for my behavior. I wanted to have what Laura had—I wanted my husband to desire, cherish, and adore me! But to actually implement what she suggested was so frightening. I didn't know if it would continue to work for me, but I knew it had worked for others, and I trusted Laura. She had restored the connection and passion in her marriage, and she had courageously and vulnerably told her story, just like I now wanted to tell mine to others.

I began learning to let go of my control and allowed my husband to manage his life, the kids, and chores, while I started taking better care of myself.

I believe God had a hand in my finding *The Surrendered Wife*, which finally led to the transformation I'd been seeking—and not just in my marriage. I realized I'd been gifted with the opportunity to heal the many years of suffering I had bottled up from my childhood by opening up and being vulnerable in my effort to save my marriage.

I dove into learning The Six Intimacy Skills head first, becoming a Surrendered Wife Trainer, and my marriage began to transform. The immediate positive response from my husband when I said "whatever you think" and Laura's encouragement gave me the confidence to continue. As I used such new skills, my heart began to soften and the fights began to diminish as I restored my dignity by apologizing when I was disrespectful.

Five years later, I also relinquished control of our finances, and when I did, my husband started making more money in his business. He even surprised me with a trip to Belize, which he planned and paid for entirely. All of the rage I'd been dumping on him soon melted away, and I was no longer on automatic angry pilot. Now I had a system: a proven set of skills that I could practice to restore the connection and intimacy immediately when I went back to my old ways, which I did from time to time.

I intuitively knew I had to help other women to continue to help myself and keep this newfound intimacy alive in my marriage. I asked my girlfriends and coworkers to support my new passion and started leading workshops in my community and coaching women by phone.

Something remarkable happened when I started sharing my story with other women: They felt safe to share their stories with me because they knew I wouldn't make them feel ashamed or judged. How could I, when I had just admitted that I had screamed at my own husband and demeaned him? I was not only saving my own marriage by telling the truth but providing a safe space for other women to begin to heal their marriages too. I experienced how telling my story could transform another life, then a community, and eventually, the world.

The secret to sharing my story was the piece of Laura's work I so admired: the willingness to be vulnerable. Being vulnerable is scary yet attractive and inviting. Sharing both the highs and lows of my experience made it possible for other women to see themselves and what might be possible for them. It provided hope, just like Laura's story did for me.

Pretending everything was okay, on the other hand, kept me not only from the vulnerability that saved my marriage but also from becoming my most authentic and best self with my husband, family, and friends. Overcoming my fear to share my story was worth it. Some friends said things like, "I had no idea you and Doug were struggling," and others cried or simply said "thank you." My marriage began to blossom, and I did too.

Before I had the courage to be seen and heard, I just hid out and pretended. I pretended nothing had happened to me as a child, taking all my pain out on my husband while acting like everything was fine to the outside world. This created a lot of internal conflict. Laura helped me see I didn't need to focus on the past. Instead, I could take small actions in my marriage that would bring about the kind of intimacy and connection I longed for—the kind I'd always craved. All along, it was my story, my pain, and my willingness to be vulnerable that would save my marriage and allow me to heal.

As a Senior Relationship Coach, I get to share my story every day. I am inspired by the women who reach out to us, just like I reached out to Laura in 2001. Women from all walks of life, faiths, and backgrounds contact us asking for support to restore the intimacy and passion in their marriages. Being continuously reminded of how my life was before I learned The Six Intimacy Skills leaves me in a state of gratitude and awe for our clients.

I'm passionate about my marriage and about what is possible for other women who are struggling, hiding, or pretending everything is fine in their relationships. I am on a mission to make it safe for every woman to tell her story and have a loving relationship. My daughters and daughter-in-law, who have followed my journey and become Surrendered Wives themselves, especially move me. They witnessed something remarkable—the saving of a marriage—and when they each married, they wanted to feel desired, cherished, and adored too. Sharing *The Surrendered Wife* and my journey authentically with my daughters and daughter-in-law, having their loving support in this work, and seeing them create intimate connection in their marriages has touched me deeply. My girlfriends, who have entrusted me with their stories and struggles, also inspire me. Their courage and openness to study the skills and even become coaches themselves is so rewarding to me.

Doug and I just celebrated our twenty-third wedding anniversary. We are more in love and connected than ever. We spend intimate moments sharing memories of raising our children and visits with our grandchildren, and we especially enjoy our coffee time together, when we ponder our future, our dreams, and the life we have today.

Doug recently came out of retirement so that I could leave my twenty-five-year career to follow my calling to become a Relationship Coach and right-hand support to Laura in her mission to end world divorce. Had I continued to pretend and not share my story or reached out for support, I wouldn't be where I am today.

My life truly is like a fairy tale! No pretending needed! Doug surprises me with trips, gifts, and compliments all the time, he manages our finances, plans for our future, and makes love to me. He is my hero and I get to be his queen!

To read more about Kathy and test your Intimacy Skills, visit: http://intimacyandpeace.com/kathy-murray/

Chapter 2

Transforming My Marriage from the Inside Out

Gladys Diaz

Senior Relationship Coach, Laura Doyle Connect

I always smile when I think about my Surrendering Journey. It's difficult for me not to see the hand of God all over my story!

I first learned about the Surrendering Principles through my sister. She had read *The Surrendered Single,* and she and a friend were inspired to contact Laura about starting a book club, to which Laura gave her blessing. *The Surrendered Single* recommends that single women select a happily married woman to be their "Married Mentor," someone they admire as a woman and wife. When my sister asked me to be not only her Married Mentor but also the Mentor for the twenty women who would be attending the book club, I had mixed emotions. Even though I was honored that my sister looked up to me and saw something in my marriage that she admired, I also knew in my heart that this marriage was not everything I had once hoped.

While my husband and I were not on the brink of divorce or separation, there was something missing in our relationship. The passion, romance, and that thing that made us *us* was no longer there. I had taken on the role of being a mother, and along the way I'd forgotten that I was also his lover. We'd fallen into a pattern of bickering and not being as romantic, passionate, or sexually intimate as we used to be. I was constantly exhausted and blamed my husband because I felt as though I had to do *everything* while he did little to support me. That deep resentment led me to withdraw physically and look for reasons to complain about just how much I was doing and how little he was doing. I didn't realize how much I had been neglecting and disrespecting my husband.

For years, our recurring argument always started with his claim that I was disrespectful towards him. I countered that he was just being overly sensitive (how disrespectful is *that*?) because, in my mind, "disrespectful" meant yelling, cursing, or throwing things at him, and I wasn't doing any of those things.

What I didn't realize was that I was constantly contradicting, questioning, and correcting my husband's ideas and decisions. I would tell him how he should speak, what he should do, and even how he should feel about things. I would complain about how he didn't help me care for our children. I didn't see my patterns, such as how, instead of asking for help with something, I'd get frustrated and just do it myself then hold it against him later.

Then, I would "encourage" him by saying things like "You could be such a great leader," "You could be making so much more money," or "You could be so successful." What I didn't know was that every time I said "You could be," all my husband would hear was, "You could be…*but you're not!*" Rather than telling him how I felt, I'd blame him for how I was feeling. If I was exhausted, I'd complain that it was because he hadn't helped me. If I felt hurt, I'd tell him how mean and insensitive he was. If I felt he was spending too much time watching TV or playing video games, I'd tell him he was immature and selfish. I was slowly chipping away at the heart and spirit of the man I had promised to love for a lifetime, and all he could see was that I'd take any opportunity to blame him or try to change him into someone else.

I decided that if I was going to mentor women in the book club, it would have to be from a better place than where we were. If I was going to serve as an example, it would be because I was actually having a loving, fun, passionate relationship with the man I'd chosen to love for life. So, I began reading *The Surrendered Single* and applying the principles in my marriage. I began dating my husband again, and I started noticing the difference in our relationship almost immediately. We were connecting more, I was being more fun and spontaneous, and there was peace in our marriage for more than just a few days at a time!

I won't lie. I liked *The Surrendered Single* a lot more than I liked *The Surrendered Wife*! In fact, I had closed the latter after reading only the introduction and quibbled that Laura had no idea what she was talking about. Clearly, I thought, this woman had no children because otherwise what she was recommending was impossible! However, as I saw the difference that reading *The Surrendered Single* had made in my marriage, I decided to pick up *The Surrendered Wife* again, and this time, I was shocked at how much Laura was describing me.

I'll never forget the day that marked our turning point. It was a Saturday and we'd spent most of the day together. Back then, I could barely speak two full sentences without saying something rude, sarcastic, or disrespectful to my husband. I started catching myself and apologizing for being disrespectful. A few times, I was able to stop myself before I said something, but mostly, I'd recognize the disrespect after the fact or, more often, mid-sentence. Each time I caught myself, I would apologize immediately. That day, I must have been on a roll because sometime in the mid-afternoon, my husband said, "You know, you don't have to keep apologizing to me."

My first reaction was to strike back and point out how he should be thankful I was being respectful (that's just the way I was back then). Instead, I turned toward him, looked him in the eyes and said, "For years, you've been telling me that I'm so disrespectful to you, and I finally see how I've been treating and speaking to you, and I agree. So, while I appreciate your saying I don't have to apologize, I do, because it's no longer okay with me to speak to you that way."

If we'd been in a cartoon, he would have been the character whose jaw drops to the floor while his eyes bulge out of his head. *That's* how shocked my husband was by what I said! After his initial shock, he gave me a look that said, "Wow! I'm not sure what just happened, but I like it. Thank you." But he simply smiled and said, "Okay."

Once I changed my own behaviors, I also noticed a big transformation in my husband. As I began admitting that I needed help and then thanking him for it, he offered to help me more often. As I began apologizing for being disrespectful in my actions and words, he took a more tender and loving approach toward me. When I began saying, "I miss you" rather than complaining that he was spending too much time on the computer or TV, he dropped what he was doing and made time for me—which was *much better* than in the past, when he'd reach for the remote and raise the volume instead!

I began feeling like the *us* we used to be was reemerging, and I felt so much closer to my husband. I also began admiring him again for the man, father, and husband he was—the man he'd always been but who I'd buried under complaints, negative expectations, and disappointments.

As the end of the three months of the Surrendered Singles Book Club drew near, we had several women in loving relationships and one who was engaged! As a special gift to the ladies, we asked Laura to surprise the women by doing a Q&A session by phone. Half way through the session, Laura asked if there was a Married Mentor in the room, and I said "yes." She said she wanted me to take the next question! I was so nervous to field a question in front of the author, but I answered it as well as I could and she loved my response. She asked me to take another question and then another, and by the end of the call, said she would love for me to be one of her coaches! Again, I was both honored and afraid because, in that moment, a dream arose in me that I could spend my life helping other women make their dreams of being in happy, peaceful, intimate relationships come true!

That invitation from Laura launched a journey that transformed not only my marriage but my life and career as well. When I began as a Surrendered Wife and Surrendered Single trainer, I was still working full-time for an education reform company, a job I had loved for over a decade but eventually held onto only because of the salary it provided for our family. However, on nights and weekends, my sister and I would coach women and lead workshops on the Surrendered Principles, and I found real happiness helping other women. After so many years as an educator and teacher-trainer, I felt called to do relationship work full-time. I must have mentioned it to anyone who would listen because, not long after, I was laid off from my job and found myself in a state of panic at what the future held for me.

The first two weeks after my layoff were dark ones laden with anxiety and fear. I could barely go more than an hour without feeling sick to my stomach or falling into a heap of sobs. I felt ashamed, even though I knew I hadn't done anything wrong, and I was terrified that I had put my family in financial jeopardy. For twelve years I had been the primary breadwinner; the layoff represented a sixty-percent loss of income for our family. A lot of people in my life responded with: "Great! Now you can finish writing your book!" or "Now you can do the relationship coaching full-time!" I knew that they were trying to encourage me, but all it did was infuriate me and make me feel that they could not comprehend what an incredible crisis my family and I were in.

One day I was in the car and my older son was excitedly talking to his little brother about his birthday party and the toy he was hoping to get. Any talk of spending money at that time triggered panic, and I started crying as soon as I parked the car in the garage. My little ones came around to my side of the car to ask what was wrong. I got out of the car, knelt at eye level with them, and told them that Mama had lost her job. My little one got very quiet, but my older son responded by getting angry and demanding that we call my boss and tell him he couldn't fire me because I worked too hard! In an effort to calm him down, I said, "Don't worry, Baby. Mama is going to find another job with better hours, where I don't have to travel as much and can do something that I love!" As soon as I said that, he wiped his eyes and smiled. "That's it, Mama! That's it! That's your new job!"

"What?" I asked him.

"That's your new job: Surrendered Wife!"

And, almost immediately, my four-year-old said, *"Don't forget Suwendered Singles!"*

The conviction with which my boys spoke was confirmation that they were speaking on behalf of someone else. I honestly felt as if God had listened to my prayers for a sign of where I should go, and, after I'd ignored what my family and friends were saying, he used the two people who I was sure to hear.

I immediately called Laura to tell her about the conversation with my boys and ask if she would mentor me in becoming a full-time relationship coach. From then on, Laura and I began partnering on different projects and ideas, such as a women's retreat. What began as a mentorship flourished into a friendship that I will treasure forever.

After nearly eight years on my Surrendering Journey, I can honestly say that I sometimes wonder if I'm living in a dream! I am a full-time relationship coach and one of Laura's Senior Relationship Coaches. Laura and I have co-hosted retreats, teleconferences, and webinars together, and I've had the opportunity to help hundreds of women around the world learn the skills they need to create the kind of relationships their hearts truly desire. I feel blessed knowing that she trusts me to help train her coaches, which is one of the most fulfilling parts of the work because I know that behind each coach I help train there are thousands of women whose hearts will be healed and whose marriages will be saved!

But to say I feel blessed is an understatement! Each day brings another opportunity to create and share love in my home and with women around the world. I take my responsibility as a relationship coach seriously. Every time a woman reaches out to me, I know that she is handing me her heart—a heart that may be filled with pain and resentment but also with the hope that she, too, can turn her relationship around. The trust, faith, and absolute courage and vulnerability that it takes for these women to reach out for help is something I never take for granted.

I am grateful to Laura for entrusting me with teaching the work she created from her own painful experiences. I admire her for having the courage to share her story and help transform the lives of women around the world.

As for my own marriage, that, too, is a dream come true! My husband and I are best friends and lovers. We have an incredibly loving and intimate marriage, and our boys get to grow up in a home that is overflowing with love and respect. In fact, one of our favorite things to do as a couple is gross them out by being romantic and mushy with one another! We strive to be positive role models and help them see what is possible for themselves and their future relationships.

I have always been an accomplished woman. In spite of a painful childhood and the loss of my first husband to cancer, I earned a full scholarship to get my degree and quickly moved up as one of the youngest female Latinas in the company where I worked for most of my adult life. My bookcase and walls are covered with awards. However, *nothing*—not one of those achievements—holds a candle to the overwhelming joy I feel when my husband speaks at one of my workshops about how my commitment to transforming myself and our marriage inspired *him* to want to become a better man. I cry every time he says it, and there hasn't been a time when a woman hasn't come up to us afterward and said, "I want my husband to speak about me the way he speaks about you!" And to think that it all started with an invitation to help *other* women experience more love in *their* lives!

To read more about Gladys and test your Intimacy Skills, visit: http://intimacyandpeace.com/gladys-diaz/

Chapter 3

Creating Lasting Intimacy

Shazia Ali

Certified Relationship Coach, Laura Doyle Connect

A relative came by a few days ago to ask me a favor. He wanted to take his wife on a surprise trip to celebrate their tenth wedding anniversary and asked if I could pick up and drop off his kids at school while they were away. I was delighted to help! I adore his little girls, and I was so impressed and happy with the romantic trip he had planned for his wife. Later that evening as I thought about their getaway, I cast my mind back on how my husband and I had spent our tenth wedding anniversary.

I remember feeling quite sorry for myself that day. A few years earlier, we'd stopped celebrating our anniversaries. But because it was the ten-year milestone, I expected my husband to make some kind of effort. In the morning, I thought I might receive a gift of some kind. I would have been happy with anything; perfume, flowers, a night out, or even some romantic words. Such a gesture would have meant that he was happy to have been married to me for ten whole years! However, the day went by, and nothing out of the ordinary happened. In fact, I had to remind him that it was our tenth anniversary. I thought to myself, "Now that I reminded him, maybe he'll go and get me something." By the time the evening came I was quite angry.

I prepared dinner, which I didn't make special in any way, and we sat down to eat. We didn't speak much during dinner, but he seemed to be enjoying himself by texting his friend and laughing at a comment he received. I remember him trying to include me in their conversation by telling me the joke, perhaps sensing that I was upset. As you can imagine, however, I didn't find it at all amusing. At that point, I was fuming and took his actions personally. I was already moody, as my suspicions had turned out to be right: He hadn't got me a gift. His lack of effort and behavior throughout our meal made me feel I was not worth the effort or time and that he was taking me for granted.

After dinner, I really felt hurt, but I wasn't one to show it, so I remained silent and told myself, "It's no big deal. We don't really celebrate anniversaries anyway." I was trying to stay calm and not say anything because I knew I would express my hurt as anger, which would result in an argument. I did express disappointment to him later in the evening because I couldn't hide it any longer, and he tried to make it up to me the next day. But I was too upset to look past my hurt to see the effort he made. Looking back, I think he enjoyed more intimacy with his friend on the mobile phone on our tenth wedding anniversary than with me.

For me, intimacy means having a strong emotional bond and being able to share things confidently, without feeling judged or dismissed. It didn't feel right that my husband preferred to be laughing with his friend when it was me he should have been sharing his time with on our special night. I thought he lacked basic relationship skills, to which I attributed how distant we had become as a couple, living almost separate lives. My reasoning was that while he may be highly involved with his job, working late nights and going abroad often, that was no excuse to stop making an effort in our marriage. I was also working part time, studying part time, and looking after the home and our two boys. I knew I wanted things to change.

I knew I wanted my husband to change, but my experience proved that I was not very successful in that area. I used to try to get him to dress better, to tidy up his paperwork and throw out things that he hadn't used in years, and to spend quality time with the children. In the beginning of our marriage, I was sometimes successful, but as time went by he started to rebel. He would wear a T-shirt without ironing it first, but if I was quick enough, I could grab it before he put it on and iron it for him. If it was too late, I would cringe at the sight of him wearing the wrinkled T-shirt and would readily tell him how sloppy he looked.

A couple of months after our uninspired anniversary, I received an email from Laura Doyle asking if I would like to become a relationship coach. The Relationship Training Course would go through all of the Intimacy Skills, which I would also have to use in my marriage throughout the course. Had God Almighty listened to my prayers? I had read Laura's book *The Surrendered Wife* a couple of years earlier, and I loved her principles. I even managed to use one of the skills, relinquishing control, in my marriage. Letting go and allowing my husband to take on responsibilities that I desperately needed help with was an amazing feeling. As for the rest of the skills, however, I thought they were great on paper but too difficult to practice in reality.

I was nervous but excited to start the course. My nerves came mostly from fear. Would these skills really work? Would my husband notice something was different? How would he respond? What if nothing changed? I even thought I would skip parts of the course where we had to practice the skills that made me the most uncomfortable, like apologizing for being disrespectful. Luckily, I didn't; I incorporated all of the Intimacy Skills in my marriage, as the course required.

Before the Coach Training Program, I thought marriage was hard work. All the experts that I was familiar with all had the same advice repeated on loop: "You have to work at your marriage!" Having two young boys to look after, a home to maintain, part-time work and education, as well as an active extended family, the last thing I had energy for was working on my marriage. Anyway, didn't it take two to tango? It didn't seem like my husband was going to try and change anything—probably because he was quite happy with the way things were.

I anxiously embarked on my journey with a group of like-minded, lovely ladies from around the globe. As I started to work through the course, it dawned on me that I had played a big part in the loneliness I felt in my marriage. Sadly, I realized that I lacked almost all of the skills that Laura talked about and wondered why I had never heard of any of them before. The first Intimacy Skill in the course was self-care, and I was confident that I knew exactly what self-care was: making myself look good for my husband, getting five pieces of fruit and veggies a day, sleeping the recommended eight to nine hours a night, and getting plenty of exercise.

To my surprise, self-care was much deeper than just making sure my basic needs were met. Self-care was about discovering who I was and what I enjoyed doing—or used to, before the husband and kids came along. Practicing self-care didn't come naturally to me, but committing to doing at least three things for myself every day made me happy and more in tune with myself. I was getting to know myself again. I felt spiritually, physically, and mentally uplifted.

Many years earlier, I had grossly violated my self-care while pregnant with my youngest child. I had never even heard of *The Surrendered Wife* and knew nothing of self-care back then. I ended up giving birth six weeks early. I hadn't even started maternity leave when my water broke. I remember texting my manager while I was in labor to say that I wasn't coming to work. The result of the baby coming early was because of lack of self-care. I kept going when I knew I should have taken it easy.

And how did I know there was a connection? A few weeks before the birth, my doctor had signed me off work because I was ill with an infection. I didn't think an infection was a good enough reason to miss work, especially with only a few weeks left until my last day. On I trudged. When my midwife said I was going to give birth six weeks early, I asked her why. Without missing a beat, she replied that early births were usually due to an infection. I felt terrible because I didn't realize until that point that I had put my baby in danger. Then, in the later stages of labor, I ignored what my body was telling me. I was always trying to do the "right" thing, even if it meant sacrificing my health. This self-righteous belief made me refuse all forms of pain relief when I obviously needed it, until my midwife spoke to me in a serious tone, saying, "We don't give medals for bravery here—take it if you need it!" I will never forget her words.

As I formed the habit of self-care, I started to feel more relaxed and to enjoy myself, enjoyment that seeped into my marriage.

Communication had also been a sore point in our marriage. I rarely let my husband finish telling me his ideas and was quick to nip them in the bud. Most of his ideas, I felt, were not worth blossoming, so I was saving time for everyone by dismissing him. I would abruptly interrupt when I heard an idea I didn't like and he would often say, "Let me finish." Let him finish? Whatever for? There was no point—after all, the idea would never become a reality! Or, I would think, "Over my dead body!" but politely say, "I don't think that's such a good idea." I believed I was protecting the family or myself from hardship. The thought of his ideas becoming reality would strike fear in me. I would envisage his ideas in my mind and play them like a movie that could only have a disastrous end: a costly project that would leave us struggling financially for years; a holiday to a country I had no interest in visiting; or a dangerous idea like allowing the children to cross a busy road by themselves (that particular idea still scares me to death). My constant nipping at him was killing the intimacy in our marriage. He stopped sharing his ideas, which I attributed to his losing interest in communicating with me.

During my journey through the Intimacy Skills, I asked myself why I was not allowing my husband to express himself fully. The honest answer that I was scared to admit to myself was that I wasn't respecting him. So at every juncture where I felt fear, I would consciously stop and ask myself what I was afraid of. Was I afraid of what he was saying? Would he ever intentionally harm me or our family? After a few days of having this internal dialogue, the truthful answer was always no. It became evident that I had to trust him more and, thankfully, the Intimacy Skills taught me how to do that beautifully. I learned that with trust comes respect. And as painful as the process was for me, I learned that having trust meant respecting his ideas too, no matter how wild they were or how afraid I felt listening to them!

I adopted the principle of respect and started hearing my husband out. I began to love listening to his ideas and thoughts, which he, very naturally, started sharing with me again. I don't often get told to let him finish, as I butt in much less. Occasionally, I still get frightened by an outrageous idea, but I have learned to take a deep breath and let him know that I hear him. By no means does that mean that I have to agree with his ideas or plans, but I can respect them. I feel comfortable knowing that it's okay if we don't agree on everything and okay to want different things in life, even though we are one team.

We have built a much deeper mutual trust. I trust that his plans are not intended to cause our family or me any hardship. If I had allowed him the opportunity to finish sharing them with me, without jumping the gun, I would have heard how his ideas were meant to enhance our lives, not make them miserable. I now see why we had a communication breakdown in our marriage.

It started to feel liberating to hear my husband talk about his ideas and not feel like I had to stop him from sharing that part of himself. It was even more empowering to express what I wanted. By simply adding the two words "I want" to a sentence, I was communicating without putting any demands on him or giving him instructions on how to go about completing tasks. I dropped any expectation of a certain outcome after telling him what I wanted, which was a little tricky to do, but I got over it because I knew how unfair it would be for me to say "Jump!" and expect him to reply "How high?" This was also liberating for me. I was no longer a slave to having to have things my way all the time, which was an exhausting mindset, as was the disappointment of things not going my way, which I could never really hide from my husband. I didn't even need to say anything to him, and he would know he hadn't done it right—again. How could my husband feel motivated to please me if I always seemed disappointed in his efforts? Is there any wonder there was distance between us?

So I started communicating what I wanted. By the grace of God, my husband has completed projects that I have been requesting for years! During the winter holidays, I expressed my desire to have a more organized space for our laundry by saying, "I really want to integrate my washing machine and dryer into a cupboard." By the end of the holidays, both appliances were neatly concealed in a brand new cupboard!

It took a lot of courage to take the initiative to get my marriage to where it is now. I may not get a medal for bravery in saving my marriage, but who needs a medal when I am rewarded by sharing intimacy with a wonderful husband every day.

From the humble beginnings when I first ordered *The Surrendered Wife* until now, as a Certified Intimacy Coach, I have never felt so empowered in my relationship with my dear husband.

To read more about Shazia and test your Intimacy Skills, visit: http://intimacyandpeace.com/shazia-ali/

Chapter 4

Finding Delight

Mari-Jean Anderson
Certified Relationship Coach, Laura Doyle Connect

Maybe my story begins last night. Sitting in my husband's office, reading by the light of a lamp balanced on a chair seat. Clark, my husband, leaned back from his desk, stretched, looked at me with a smile full of love, contentment, and desire. That sweet smile was bigger and more important to me than the scattered laundry, the tattered couch, and his mother in the living room blasting the seven millionth episode of *Blue Bloods* on TV. It is the beginning of my story because I'm excited to get to the next part! And the next and the next.

When I say that I am excited to be with my husband, that is the absolute truth. He pleases me in so many ways, and I feel satisfied and at peace when I am with him. Surrendering is definitely not a static position. There are good days, great days, and days that I am teetering on the brink of murder, but on all days, good and bad, I am confident that I have the tools to get myself back to happiness. Surrendering has taught me that I have control over one thing and one thing only: how I manage myself. You may be wondering, "Why does that matter when my husband is the problem?" Listen closely—I'm going to tell you the world's best and worst kept secret: How you manage yourself is all that matters. Wait! Give me a moment before you turn away in disgust. I was where you are, or based on many conversations with unhappy women, I was very close to where you are.

Clark and I met and married in our fifties. He was a confirmed bachelor. This was my third marriage, the other two totaling less than three years and the last one having dissolved several decades earlier. We found we had so much to talk about; we saw eye to eye on family, religion, politics, money, and our children. We never had so much as a raised voice throughout our courtship. Our friends and family saw us as a great couple. We both had good lives, sufficient finances, and plenty of experience in the dating world.

We married, and it all changed. Just like that. The man who used to drive more than one hundred miles round trip to see me didn't move in until six weeks after the wedding. The thought-provoking conversations that we used to have in the hot tub under the stars— gone. He was too busy, too tired, too anything in the world to sit with me under the night sky.

Those delicious nights of lovemaking became a faded memory, and the kisses disappeared along with them. He'd come home from work and go directly into his office without saying hello; he'd leave without saying goodbye. He never fixed anything, never picked up after himself, never held me in the night or called me in the day. Shall I go on? He never brought me flowers, gifts, or planned a night out. He didn't help in the garden or fix my car, and the question of walking the dog was an argument in the making. He hated any discussion about home improvements or repairs.

The more he withdrew, the harder I pushed. I came from a background of "Don't complain, suck it up, make it work." This had always worked great for me in business. Marriage? Not so much. I could not figure out what was going on.

I was frantic; I felt lost and betrayed. I was ashamed to have been so stupid to marry him. I'd had such a great life, and now it had turned into a pile of hopeless misery. I was too embarrassed even to tell anyone what was going on. I could barely admit it to myself, much less anyone else. We looked good from the outside but inside? I cried myself to sleep on many occasions.

He had an opportunity go overseas for a year, leaving me at home, and we both leaped at the chance. I saw it as a time to regroup and figure out what to do, to reconnect and fall in love again, long distance. I'd always known how to get things done, and I made the commitment that I'd get this marriage working again. I worked like a crazy person getting all our half-started projects finished. We had a few rental properties. Everything got fixed, painted, and put on the market. I was going to do this! I would get everything done that my husband didn't, including fixing our relationship. I would be the best left-behind wife ever. I wrote at least once a week and sent packages regularly. When he called, I perkily told him about all the things I was finishing up. I believed in the mantra "We mustn't upset our men when they are overseas" and stuck to it. It never occurred to me that there were actually two people in this marriage.

I felt more and more lost as the year turned into thirty months and the gulf between us was leagues wider than the miles. The only letter I ever received was an email he copied to his siblings. He called almost every day but didn't respond to my emails, and I had no way to reaching him if I needed to talk.

Eventually he came home, road weary and more than a little off from being in wartime Afghanistan. We both declared that it was going to be different this time and moved to Tampa for his new position. In a sense, everything looked better. I'd sold off all our properties, so there was nothing I needed him to help me with.

There was also nothing for me to do.

I put my energies into becoming a housewife. Have you ever seen a border collie at work with her sheep? That is how I must have looked to him when I did housework, full of neurotic, hyper-focused energy. He became more absent than ever. He had little interest in moving into our new home, decorating, or exploring the neighborhood. He never cooked, cleaned up after himself, or shopped for food. Why should he? Anything he did, I re-did.

One day I was Googling marriage counselors and divorce and found a piece about Laura Doyle and the book *The Surrendered Wife*. I was desperate for any kind of help—or maybe just looking for a way to confirm my marriage was hopeless and I should get divorced—so I bought the book. The title was a little embarrassing. *Surrendered*? It sounded like some religious cultish thing, so I hid the book, reading it only in the bathroom. Good thing it was short!

What Laura said made some sense to me, but I thought most of it was written for someone else. After all, I thought, I wasn't the problem—my husband was. I was already doing everything. He simply had to change a few things, like I asked him to, and we'd be okay. I look back at that time with amazement. How could I not know that my husband had his own feelings, his own ideas, and his own comforts that were separate from mine? I didn't ask, and he didn't tell. His love for me and for keeping peace kept him quiet and agreeable.

The first thing from the book that I put into practice was to stop buying him clothes and dressing him. It drove me crazy that he'd wear khaki Dockers and a blue dress shirt every work day, a Hawaiian shirt and khaki shorts for the weekends. I knew if he'd just wear the much more fashionable clothing I bought for him, he'd see how much better he looked. I was pompous enough to think that if I introduced this fifty-five-year-old world traveler to things I thought were great, he'd realize they were great too. I remember one time I thought I'd gotten him the best, most extravagant gift ever: three pairs of cashmere socks. I was drooling over them. The following year, I went into his drawers, took the unopened socks, and started wearing them myself. *I'd* always wanted cashmere socks. How could *he* not want them? Once I learned to listen without judgment, I learned that he sees himself, in his words, as "a simple Midwesterner." Extravagance embarrasses him.

He's kind and generous with me in his own way, but I had to learn to stop talking and to listen to him in order to understand that. I remember my first birthday with my husband. We had been married about six months and he hinted that he'd found just the right thing for me. When the day came, I excitedly opened a beautifully wrapped little box to find ... a Garmin. A GPS for my car. I was devastated. It took years before I understood his heart message: Since I spent much of the day driving, this was a gift I would use every day. This was a gift that honed in perfectly on what I needed. It gave me a guaranteed route to get me where I needed to go and to guide me home every night. I cheated myself when I didn't stop to understand that, and I cheated him of the joy of watching me receive graciously something that would sweeten my life. After all, it was the man's version of cashmere socks, wasn't it? No wonder he stopped giving me presents. I didn't appreciate how he was telling me he loved me.

Next, I began to stay out of his social conversations. I stopped trying to teach him how to leave a message, how to talk to his family, how to speak to his friends (alas, I really did do that) and lo and behold, nothing bad happened.

Then, I began leaving his office and his car alone. I stopped tidying up his room and making his office more efficient. I remember having an intense internal debate about whether to open the shutters in his office, but I persevered and left his things alone. Just recently we were talking and I mentioned the closed shutters. He told me (and he can tell me now because I don't interrupt) that after spending thirty months in a war zone, the open windows made him nervous. Holy Christmas! Who knew? It makes me so happy to know he can confide in me now; I feel like we are on the same team. And yes, he is okay with my sharing his story with you too.

Once I stopped trying to control his clothes, his office, and his thoughts, I began to see a difference. I don't know how he felt, but I was suddenly released from an awful lot of self-imposed responsibility. And you know what? Nothing collapsed. He never ran out of gas or had to go to work naked, and he didn't miss his appointments or get lost.

About six months into the process, Laura sent an invitation to join her training session and become an Intimacy Coach. I spoke with her on the phone and was infected by her good will, her energy, and her absolute belief in what she was doing. "Besides," she said, "think of it as an investment in your own marriage!" I would appreciate again and again how true that statement was. I've come to believe that being in a great and loving marriage is more valuable than almost anything! I decided to go ahead and start training to become a Coach.

With so many defense mechanisms in place, it was hard to hear things about myself objectively. An important aspect of the Coach Training was the actual coaching that took place each week, when one trainee volunteered to act as the coach and one as the client. Listening to this live demonstration opened my eyes and ears. Early in the course, I'd find myself making snap judgments based on my old rulebook. I had the answers ready before the client finished her sentence. Often the coach took a completely different track than I thought of, and when I saw how right it ended up being, my heart began to open. I began to understand that coaching isn't about telling someone what to do; it's about listening. It's about believing in that client's ability to know what is right for her. Talk about giving up control!

As I progressed in the training, I learned about the other wonderful, strong, and competent women in the group. We laughed, cried, bared our souls and our hearts. We'd found a place to express our real selves and lives, knowing we were safe and accepted and that nothing was too awful to share. The more we shared our differences, the more we recognized our similarities. Listening to another woman with the same issues as me made it so much easier to understand what was really going on in my own life. I found that, no matter how we look, sound, or dress, we all want much the same things. We want to be loved and respected and to feel we make a difference.

Reporting on my progress practicing the Skills for homework was grueling because I knew someone who had been where I was would hold me accountable for what I said. Someone who would be kind, understanding, and would see through every excuse I made. When I read the book, you'd better believe I knew everything. But as a student accountable to a group of like-minded women, not so much. I began to take a long, hard look at myself.

As ridiculous as it sounds now, I had no idea what a control freak I was then. I really saw myself as a person who wanted to help others by paving the way with ideas. Ideas that were mine and so full of explicit instructions that there was no room for discussion. No wonder my husband hated having discussions about what needed to be fixed around the house. Those sessions were simply a platform for me to tell him how to do things. I'm mortified to realize how demeaning my "help" was. It was insulting to my husband and exhausting for me.

Another upside of surrendering is the conscious release of all those things that we don't have control over anyway. Poof, the responsibility is gone. Now when I ask Clark what he thinks, he knows I mean it. He tells me. When I make myself shut up and listen, really listen, to what he is saying, I'm impressed again and again with his knowledge and understanding. He gets to his answers in such a different way than I do that it is always a revelation. I'm delighted to find that, once I understand what he is talking about, I often fully agree. Now, Clark is willing to discuss projects that I'm thinking about. He often has a completely different take on them with even better solutions than I could have imagined. What a treasure trove of information! It is a testament to his love and patience that he didn't press a pillow over my face until I stopped telling him what to do.

Then, the homework instructed me to thank my husband three times a day for something that he did for me. This was early in the program, when I figured this stuff could work for other people but wouldn't really work for me. I couldn't even think of three things to thank him for, so I decided just to use the examples that Laura gave in the training. My mouth felt dry as I uttered the first ridiculous statement: "Sweetheart, I just want to thank you for going to work every day." I still can't believe how hard it was to get those words out. I knew he would fall down laughing or see the lie for what it was and walk out. Instead, he told me how happy it made him to be able to take care of me. I'd never equated his going to work with a desire to take care of me. I figured he had worked before he met me and continues to work now. Suddenly, I realized that his going to work was another way of showing he loved me.

That was the beginning of the Great Thaw.

I once lived someplace up north where part of the winter entertainment was to push an old car onto a frozen lake and make bets as to what day the ice would melt enough to let the car fall through. It made me examine the frozen lake in a different way if I could see the day it started to melt. This was that day for our relationship.

Since discovering *The Surrendered Wife* and completing the Coach Training Program, I've become a kinder, happier person. I feel free not to do the things I don't want to. My husband loves me. He really, really does. He tells me by his actions and now, more and more, by his words. I've learned to express what I want in a way that makes him want to do it for me.

It's not all smooth sailing though. Six months ago his invalid mother moved in with us, needing round-the-clock care. The needs of this tiny woman have enveloped our entire house, our time, and our privacy. When we decided to invite her to live with us, I told him that I'd need his help around the house. One of the things that makes me so insane that I fear my head will spin around and pea soup will spew out of my mouth is this: He doesn't know what to do to help. I no longer try to figure out what it is he is thinking or feeling; I've learned I'm not a mind reader. Instead, this is what I do: I tell him exactly what I want.

Now, he makes the bed every morning and does the final cleanup before we go to bed at night. Those two things have changed my world. When I wake up, the kitchen is clean; I walk back to the bedroom and it looks great. I tell him all the time how happy it makes me. I tell him it makes me feel like he really loves me. "But I do," he says. "I really do love you!" "Well," I tell him, "this really shows it to me. Every time I walk in the room, I'm reminded." You can bet he hasn't missed a day in over six months!

Our marriage, our partnership, grows stronger and more alive every day. With his mother staying with us, our private time has temporarily been reduced to random bits and pieces, but now I have a contentment and satisfaction that I hadn't thought possible. Most importantly, on those days that I can remember nothing good and have completely lost my way, I have a system that works and the tools to get back on track.

Is my husband the perfect man I dreamed of? Don't be ridiculous. But he is still the man I married—the one who loves me and cares for me with everything he is capable of, who is in my corner when I need backup, and who seems to forgive me for anything. He's there in the dark of night, the light of day, and when my nose is dripping or I have a pimple. I have learned, finally, to love him for what he is and for what he isn't, for what he brings, for what he lets go of. I love him for who he is and for who I am when we are together. I never knew what a real partnership could be. It's a wonder. This too I've learned: Not much in life is perfect, nor will it ever be. But be delighted. Even if it's not perfect, be delighted and eventually, you will find your delight to be perfectly true.

To read more about Mari-Jean and test your Intimacy Skills, visit: http://intimacyandpeace.com/mari-jean-anderson/

Chapter 5

The Pursuit of Happiness

Norita Bonin

Certified Relationship Coach, Laura Doyle Connect

"For better or worse, for richer or poorer, in sickness and in health." I did not think I was signing up for worse, poorer, and sickness all at once. I spent thirty years in this unhappy place until I learned the Intimacy Skills from Laura Doyle. Now, I am enjoying the better, richer, and health parts of my vows, and I am so happy we stayed in our marriage.

When I was fourteen and my future husband was seventeen, my older sister planned a weekend get-together for teenagers at our parents' farm. He attended with his close friend and we fell head over heels in love. The first kiss swept me off my feet. It felt stunning to be passionately kissed and pursued, and so began a courtship that lasted over six years.

We loved to be together as often as possible and talked on the phone once a week, even though it was expensive in those days. It was great when my sister moved to the city where he lived and I would visit every few months. He also came to visit me at the farm. The dinner dates, sweet time with our families, romantic walks, and kisses in the moonlight were straight out of a storybook. I loved being kissed, cuddled, and wooed for hours on end. And the story lasted for years.

Once we were both old enough, we got married. As we returned from the honeymoon and started our life together, we were busy, both working full time. I assumed I would take care of the bills and manage the money because that's what my mom had done when I was growing up. Hindsight tells me that was my first wrong turn. Though he never said anything, I believe my well-intentioned actions made my husband physically sick. Six weeks into our marriage, he became ill. He was in bed for weeks. I was so scared. I did not feel secure in his ability to support me. We had agreed I would keep my job for one year so we could save money to travel overseas before having children. Once we accomplished our savings goal and took our trip, I was afraid to quit my job because there wasn't enough money to pay the bills and I was afraid his health was not good enough for him to work.

After we had been married a little over a year, my husband took over some foreclosure rental properties, and we worked together fixing them up. I resented that he was not a good provider and I had to do so much. We had several mortgages for the rental properties, but we didn't own them—they owned us. We both worked full time and took care of the rental properties in the evenings and on weekends.

The first child came at year five. Now, I also had full responsibility for child-rearing, as well as homemaking and yard care. I was beyond stretched and one very angry woman! This was not what I had envisioned for myself when I said marriage vows.

Our regular routine was that I would make my husband's breakfast and lunch. We wore out three high-quality waffle irons because he wanted homemade waffles every day. I then packed him a giant, homemade lunch and a variety of drinks. He was in construction and needed a lot of food to keep going. When I didn't pack his lunch or make him a full breakfast, he would fail to feed himself then get too weak to function. As the years rolled by with no relief, I felt weary of being a slave to his stomach. When I came home from work at night, I went straight to making dinner while he read the newspaper or a novel. I also did the laundry and tended to the lawn.

While he sat there reading, my resentment grew to unmanageable proportions. I could not understand why he didn't help me. Quite often, I would leave the house in angry silence to work on our rental properties after dinner. He might or might not join me later, but when he did, we would work in silence, quietly resenting each other. I could not understand why he avoided me, resisted helping me, and didn't talk to me. Couldn't he see how much I was sacrificing? Why did he care for me so little that he would just leave everything for me to handle?

Then I would stay up late into the night paying bills and keeping the household running. When I was completely exhausted, I would fall into bed, but he still wanted one more thing! Even making love felt like a chore. Finally, when all of my chores were complete, I could fall asleep for a few hours before starting all over again. I despaired about how things had turned out. I was overwhelmed and exhausted but didn't know what else to do but suck it up and power through.

The rentals were not making money or letting us break even, so I couldn't quit my job. I started a home business while I was still working so I could continue to make money while staying home to raise our children. Because of my husband's poor health and physically demanding career, I feared mine would become the main source of income at any time.

For the next several years, I built a few different home businesses in an attempt to keep the rentals afloat. The intensity of feeling overwhelmed and resentful lessened once I quit my full-time job to operate my home businesses, but those feelings never went away. I felt vulnerable because I was uncertain whether he would be able to keep working, and I knew my home business income alone would not support us. I felt resentful because I was a workhorse but my work ethic went unappreciated.

Because of the great sorrow and emotional pain, my body was weakening. Regularly I welcomed my death. I was not suicidal, but I wanted my misery to end. Because of my faith and the vow "until death do us part," I knew death was my only way out. I sought escape by sleeping a lot. I could no longer keep up the pace or get much done. My sister voiced her concern that it looked like I was headed for a major health crisis, and I turned to alternative medicine for help. I regained strength as my blood pressure and heart issues resolved.

For our twenty-fifth anniversary, we went to Seattle and stayed at a nice hotel I had won as a door prize at a networking meeting. When we arrived, my husband settled into a chair to read. I went to bed and quietly cried myself to sleep, with him knowing nothing of my sadness. We rarely took trips without our kids, and when we did it was like this. I could barely endure the neglect. A year or so later, my husband was going to travel for training and asked me to go. I could not bear to go with him again. My expectations of intimacy were higher when we were on trips than at home but would still go unmet. I wanted to be romanced and have his attention, but he would read or watch TV instead. The pain of rejection was too great, so rather than go with him, I went to visit my parents and sister.

When we both returned home, the short break had given me the strength to finally open up to him. I told him that I didn't like how our routine of quick sex felt more about him than me and that I did not feel satisfied. My dissatisfaction with our sex life wasn't new; that went way back to when we first made love. But I didn't say anything—just waited. And waited. And waited.

Over the years, I had read books about how to make it better, but they really didn't help, and I was too embarrassed to ask anyone else. Early in our marriage, I suspected that if I were given enough time and attention, all would be well, but I wanted him to *want* to give me that attention freely, without my having to ask for it.

Once I finally told him how I felt, he was very upset and thought I had disclosed this to my family on my recent visit. I reassured him that it had nothing to do with my family and that I hadn't mentioned it, but he remained unconvinced, wanting to know why it had come up right after my trip. I explained that this was something I had struggled with from the beginning of our marriage but that I had never known what to do about it. Still, it took years for him to move past his angry reaction.

When we had been married about twenty-seven years, I started practicing living a life of gratitude, which improved our relationship to a degree. I no longer allowed my negative thoughts to run away with me. It was by no means the life I had dreamed of, but by now it was manageable. I silently recommitted to staying in the marriage, regardless of whether I was happy or not. As I considered all the people in my life and how much they would be hurt by our breakup, I decided I would take the "hit" and remain in the marriage. I told myself I was enduring for just this life and that my real happiness would come on the other side of the grave.

One day, just before I learned the Intimacy Skills, my demeanor slipped. While I was usually pretty even keeled by this time, on this particular day my husband's usual way of leaving the house in silence made me angry. Once again I felt like I had taken all I could and called my daughter to vent. My dear daughter had known all along about our difficult marriage but still maintained a great friendship with both of us. She had been married a few years by then and her own marriage wasn't all she expected either. When we spoke, she confided that she had read this amazing book but feared that telling me might compromise our relationship, especially once I heard the title. Yet on this day, she took the risk of losing my friendship and revealed to me the book *The Surrendered Wife* by Laura Doyle. I am so grateful that she did because it changed my course and was exactly what I needed. She told me she had read the book without telling her husband so she would have the space to learn without him expecting too much too soon. I decided I would do the same. I needed that time to learn without pressure.

The first skill I implemented was relinquishing control by saying "whatever you think." Then I learned about respect and saying "I hear you." Little by little, things began to improve. When I finished *The Surrendered Wife*, I said to myself, "Parts of this do not work for me. I have these rentals to run, and it is my job. I can't relinquish control of the finances." However, my next thought was, "I could just try it, and if it does not work I could go back." So that evening after my husband returned from work, I said, "I can't manage our money anymore. I don't think I've done a very good job at it, and I am frustrated." He agreed I hadn't done a good job but was not pleased when I relinquished control of this monumental task. For the next year, he tried to push parts of it back onto me. I continued to say "I can't" and thanked him for taking care of things for us. He eventually saw that we did not have enough income to pay our bills and began making more money and being a good provider.

At some point, I felt my skills slipping and wanted a refresher, so I went online to see if there was a website. I read Laura's blog, signed up for the newsletter, and clicked the button about coach training. Thinking I would get some automated response, I was surprised when I got a phone call the next day from Kathy Murray, a Senior Relationship Coach with Laura Doyle. As I listened to Kathy talk about coach training, I said, "I like what you're telling me, but I can't do one more thing. I am already too busy with my home business and managing our rental properties. I was just curious." I continued, "It's not realistic to think I could do one more thing. I would be crazy to consider it. And anyway, I've never even told my husband about reading the book, and I have relinquished control of the finances, and I feel pretty certain we don't have the money…" On and on I went. Kathy listened for a while before she suggested some ways I could approach my husband about coaching.

When I asked him if he had noticed any positive changes in our relationship recently, he said yes and my heart did a happy leap. Then I told him, "I read a book without telling you and implemented some new skills to see if they would make a difference for me, and they did. Then I found out about an opportunity to become a certified relationship coach. I would love to do this! I will go with whatever you think because you are the head of our household." He had about ten questions I had not thought to ask Kathy, so the next day, after speaking with her again, I answered his questions.

One of the painful things that had happened in our marriage is that no matter what I asked, he would either take a long time to answer or, more frequently, not answer. For the most part, I learned to quit asking because I would be hurt; instead, I just took charge of what I wanted. However, this time I expressed what I wanted and added, "whatever you think." He came to me thirty minutes later to say, "You may sign up for the training."

After a few months of coach training, I started to catch on to the skills, especially learning how to say what I want. I used to manipulate without even realizing it, but through coaching I got the tools to change, including honoring my desires. Laura teaches that saying what we want purely and clearly is the essence of femininity. It is quite vulnerable to do this because even if I say what I want, I must let go of expectations of when or how my desires are met. I can hope and I can say it again, as long as I don't say the word *you*. I stay on my own paper and keep myself happy, even if I don't get what I want. Once I started implementing the skill of expressing my desires purely, I realized for the first time since being married that I was treasured, cherished, and adored.

One of the missing pieces I found through coaching is that men truly want to make women happy. I've lived most of my life the opposite way, as I thought it was my job to make him happy. Since I started being happy and saying so, I am constantly grateful for all the things he does for me. Astonishing! Even something small, like a tender meeting of our eyes, is such a rewarding and beautiful experience. I am so happy he wants to be with me! What a contrast to the pain of being avoided.

Reading Laura's book then training as a coach revealed that the biggest missing piece all these years was happiness. In the bad old days, it seemed that my entire household was full of long faces desperately trying to avoid eye contact. It is lonely and painful to live that way, and no big house is big enough for unhappy people. Now, we are a house full of happy, smiling, hugging people. We seek each other out. We laugh at each other's jokes. We have fun. Friends have even been asking what happened because they also see the changes. My husband says, "When people hear my wife is a relationship and intimacy coach, they wonder what the husband's perspective is. I'm here to tell you, it works."

Another wonderful side effect of implementing the skills in my marriage is the positive impact it has had on my relationship with my children. We have a teenage son taking drivers ed. He was approaching a stop sign too fast. Before the Intimacy Skills, I used to tell him to slow down, and he would argue about his ability to control the car. Now I say, "I want to feel safe." That's it—no more arguing—and he slows down the way I like. I often tell him what a good driver he is, and I mean it. The other night, when the sprinklers were still running, my son went into the backyard to turn them off without even being asked. I thanked him and added, "Did you also turn off the ones in the front?" When he said no, I said I would go do it. He headed upstairs for bed but then turned around and, without saying anything, went to the front yard to turn them off. I am so happy to have a fifteen-year-old son treating me like this. We also have an older son who, for years, insisted he would never marry—a result of being raised by unhappily married parents. Now that our marriage has become so great, he says, "I will only get married if I can find someone like Mom."

Years ago, before surrendering, I was prompted to write down what I would truly love to do—even if I didn't make money at it or had no idea of how to accomplish it. I wrote, "I would love to help couples find happiness in their marriages." I laughed to myself when I wrote this. How could I help someone else when I didn't have a happy marriage myself? Now as a relationship coach, I hear heartbreaking stories from other women, and memories of how my relationship was before coaching come flooding back. Because of my own unhappiness for so many years, I can look into the faces of other women, even strangers, and know just what they are going through. I wasted so much time being in that place, and now I am on a mission to help others find their bliss. Too many women are not happy yet. I did not know it was within my power to make a difference, but Laura Doyle taught me skills to change my life while allowing me to fulfill my dream of helping other women find happiness in their relationships too.

To read more about Norita and test your Intimacy Skills, visit: http://intimacyandpeace.com/norita-bonin/

Chapter 6

Saving a Stressed Marriage from Divorce

Sheri Byrd

Certified Relationship Coach, Laura Doyle Connect

"Surely from this period of ten months this is the lesson: never give in, never give in, never, never, never—in nothing, great or small, large or petty—never give in except to convictions of honor and good sense." —Winston Churchill

Today, after nearly thirty years of marriage to the original man of my dreams, I am loved, cherished, treasured, adored, and supported. He is affectionate and romantic. I am emotionally strong and set clear boundaries.

It wasn't always so.

As the wife of a soldier turned civilian federal law enforcement officer for twenty-six years, my marriage had its share of stresses: deployments, moving thirteen times in the first twenty years, raising toddlers alone, surviving in difficult places far from family. I thought I had the stress under control. I was a third-generation military wife, for heaven's sake, and *I got this*. I knew how to take over every detail of our domestic life, even during a major move, and run a tight ship, making everything fall into place one way or another. I'd had an accomplished career as a journalist and public relations director. I'd been a stay-at-home mom for eleven years. I'd taught dance and aerobics and had run a half marathon. I was living the dream I was told makes modern women happy: having it all.

So why was I miserable? Why did I feel nothing but inadequate? I was depressed, and efforts on my husband's part to cheer me up, please me, or even touch me, I took as merely obligatory. I considered it his job to do what I wanted him to, act how I liked all day every day, and attract me too. I wanted to live a certain way, do certain things, make the house look the way I wanted it. It was so hard do it all by myself, but my husband seemed to have no interest in helping me! If something was going to be done, it was up to me. I would tell him exactly what to do and why it should be done. When he didn't want to do things as I said, I would cry and say, "That is not the way to treat someone you love!"

I believed if he didn't see things my way, he was not loving me. What I didn't see was that I was doing the same thing to him. I felt like I couldn't do anything well enough to make myself or anyone in my family happy. I cried all the time and blamed my husband for making me feel so bad and for not caring. Yet I felt like the only adult in the house and was stretched beyond my capacity to care for myself, my marriage, my home, or my family. Any suggestions of self-care just felt like one more thing I should do, one more thing on my endless list of obligations. No way. And when it came to the bedroom, I didn't think I was that attractive with my few extra pounds, so I did not believe my husband's affection had anything to do with actually loving me. I never doubted my husband was the man for me, but I just couldn't stop crying or being frustrated by him. I feared the only way we could be happy together was for me to tamp down my feelings with strong medical prescriptions.

For our twentieth anniversary, he surprised me and our two teenagers with a trip to Hawaii. He had planned the whole thing. That was unheard of and what I'd been asking for years! But instead of being happy and excited, I was upset. He had planned the trip for just after our holiday-season anniversary, when the rates dropped in mid-January. "What were you thinking," I asked him. "The kids can't miss a whole week of school!" So he canceled the vacation and took me to dinner.

We promised we'd go some other time.

After more than twenty years of marriage, he turned cold and distant. We tried marriage counseling, briefly. He felt the therapist ambushed him, focusing on what he was doing wrong and how he should change. Both of us could see it was not helping and soon quit. I believed what the women around me said based on what the vast majority of them had experienced: I had only two solutions— stronger anti-depressants or divorce.

He chose for both of us, and we soon separated. In my typical "I got this" way, I hit the Internet, grasping for solutions: marriage help, divorce prevention, etc. After a labyrinth of links, I landed on a review of *The Surrendered Wife*, by Laura Doyle. I read about marriages that were not only saved but revolutionized! One phrase stopped my breath for just a moment, resonating so deeply I could not ignore it: "Women hold the power in relationships. Learn the skills to have a good marriage, practice them, and like produce from a well-tended garden, a good marriage will likely follow," the review said. A voice in my heart whispered, "You hold the power." I bought *The Surrendered Wife* in print, audio, and digital versions. I knew I needed more help to fit the principles to my own situation and consulted one of Laura Doyle's relationship coaches. The following months were like a zero-to-hero movie montage as I learned, practiced, and strengthened skill after skill, receiving personal coaching along the way to fit my specific marital issues. I had setbacks, but the relationship coaching included how to handle those with forgiveness, grace, and dignity.

The next year was both the most joyful and most painful of my life. Through reading *The Surrendered Wife,* practicing the skills, and relationship coaching, I learned the deep joy of true self-care, drastically decreasing my stress level and increasing the peace of maintaining my dignity through the emotional storms raging around me. Even through ten months of separation and five more months "dating" my husband back into my life, I never gave up. I never wanted to. I knew I loved this man as much or more than I ever had, and I would never give up as long there was a spark of hope. I could not let my marriage and my family go, no matter how much I was hurting, without being certain that I had done everything I possibly could to save it. That transitional year was difficult, watching our whole family in such pain, and I could have just walked away at any point, but, thank heaven, I persevered. If I had not, there is zero doubt that my marriage would now be long since over, our family ripped apart.

If I could give advice to the controlling young woman I was on my wedding day, congratulated and respected by so many for being "strong," I would say *love* is an action verb, not just a feeling. I would say, "Honey, you must put your love into every word, every tone, and every action to keep it alive. If your husband says it, he means it; don't try to mind-read. Listen to his dreams, and don't worry, fight, or even quibble over anything that has not yet happened. Give him problems to be fixed, not orders to follow. Accept his gifts, help, and compliments as a sign of his love in action. Reject the gifts, and you reject the giver. Men need respect like they need oxygen; give him that and he'll give you the world. Deny him that and suffocate the relationship."

I'm still working on inspiring my husband. When he is stressed, he retreats, like many men, in order to replenish himself. If I'm visibly happy, he's less stressed and more inclined to help and to be open to fun. It took some time for me to see the skills I was learning were really working. My husband was so far out the door, it took a while for him to get close enough to notice, much less to trust, the changes in me. After about three months of my new behaviors, he told me he doubted if it was just a temporary change and that he didn't know if he wanted to continue pursuing divorce. I knew the seeds of a new relationship were sprouting.

Before our crisis, I had no specific or major issues with him; it was the little daily things that made me so miserable—and that now make me so happy. Just recently, he knew I needed to get some work done from home but also needed to go grocery shopping for dinner with our kids that night. All I said was, "I wish the weekend were longer; I have too much to do today." He jumped in with an offer to do the shopping. I happily accepted, and he brought home my whole list, plus fresh sourdough bread, three cases of wine on sale (after rebates, which he promptly processed), and a full tank of gas. His love in action.

I learned the skills to be my very best self, not the "perfect" version in the world's eyes. Without the same old me, we could not be the same old us! I became a better me, and after a while, *we* became a better *us*!

I receive! Graciously! Whether he brings me a new car or a cup of tea, I receive with true appreciation for every gift, just as it is. Appreciation not just felt but skillfully shown. I smile warmly and say, "Thank you, honey!" every time he takes out the trash or mows the lawn. Before, I'd have snipped, "What? You want a medal for basic responsibility?" And you know what? He helps more and thanks *me* more too.

I show respect. My tone of voice and choice of words matter. He wants to take a route I wouldn't choose? That's his choice and I respect it. He wants a car I wouldn't have even considered? He has that right, and I respect his desires, from dinner options to retirement dreams. Often, his way turns out better than anything I'd have come up with!

I choose to give up control. Why? The only person I can ever really control is myself. My husband knows how to take care of his own needs. Nagging is not helping, as I once thought. I have learned the value of what does not need to be said. My former efforts to "help" were like termites to the house of our marriage. One didn't do much damage, but many, over time, destroyed our intimacy. Now, when I am stressed and snap, "No, I did not plan anything for dinner. Did you?" I realize that my mood is my responsibility, and if I've gotten that bad, I've let myself get depleted.

My husband has always complimented me, telling me how beautiful I am and how lucky he is to have me. For years, decades even, I didn't believe him. I had thoughts about myself and my image from childhood that I just couldn't shake. Then in my thirties, I started gaining weight despite a healthy lifestyle. I felt awful and saw his compliments only as an attempt to get me in the mood, which I also did not equate with love. I would deflect his compliments. Now, I smile and say, "Thank you, sweetie," every time!

I choose to be vulnerable. Like someone falling backwards into the arms of a friend playing trust fall, I choose to trust my husband every day, and he rises to the occasion. I skillfully express my feelings and desires, releasing any expectations of the outcome. And he is more considerate, affectionate, and romantic, planning more vacations and date nights and spontaneous fun than ever in our twenty-seven years of marriage!

I used to be so disrespectful. My husband likes country music. For years, I'd curl my lip in a disgusted sneer and leave the room when he turned on a country station, particularly when he was getting ready in the morning or driving. He'd just sigh sadly and say, "You don't like me." I'd insist that of course I liked him; I just didn't like country music! I've since apologized for all those times I made fun of his music, and I even started listening to some country artists I liked, singing along when we were both home. He said he was very glad I'd opened up to it. Then he switched all the stations to classic rock. It wasn't easy because I like soft rock and New Age, but I had to learn to respect that too.

After I shared my story, Laura Doyle called to ask me to join the first class of her newly redesigned Coaching Program. She said she hadn't trained anyone in over six years, and I was at the top of her list. The investment was enough to give me pause. I wanted it so badly though. I told my husband what I wanted, without including my long list of logical reasons. I only told him how much it would mean to me. My thrifty husband replied, "You have to do this."

The new skill that still takes real effort is remembering that when I feel resentment or irritation with *him*, it's up to *me* to get some fun, pleasurable self-care ASAP and not fall into focusing on his faults. Happily, such irritation is very rare now that gratitude and self-care take center stage in my life. Once, when my husband was stressed out over work and chronic back pain, we had been watching TV together and he left the room during a commercial to get a drink. I told him I would pause the show when it restarted. However, I started surfing social media on my phone and got distracted. He returned to find the show had been back on for several minutes. He exploded, "What is wrong with you?" This was very out of character for him, and I knew it was just an accumulation of recent stress. Nonetheless, it wasn't okay, and I wasn't okay. I let the tears show and simply said "ouch." I got up calmly and left the room. I poured a bath and took a good long soak. When I got out, he said, "I'm so sorry. I'll try to do better," and gave me a huge hug. I said, "Thank you, sweetie."

Before I surrendered control of him and his life, he appeared to me as an overgrown child. I couldn't see all of his accomplishments and tireless efforts providing for our family. Now, he appears no less than heroic to me. His humor, caring, and sense of responsibility fill me with awe and appreciation. His little words of fun and affection make me love him more every day.

To read more about Sheri and test your Intimacy Skills, visit: http://intimacyandpeace.com/sheri-byrd/

Chapter 7

My Beautiful, Blessed, Bittersweet Love Story

Darlene Davis

Certified Relationship Coach, Laura Doyle Connect

We never know what the outcome will be, so all we can do is take the chance and give it all we've got with no regrets!

My love story began in 1976 when a girlfriend and I were cruising around a shopping center, like most teenagers did back then. The door of a mysterious green Mustang opened and out *he* came, a tall, lean Indian, with proud high cheekbones and long dark hair. I watched him walk across the parking lot with a long, smooth stride and a confidence that was obvious. I was almost sixteen, a tomboy who knew nothing about love, but my heart jumped and my eyes lit up. It was love at first sight. So I did what a teenager does: I left a silly note on his windshield telling him I liked him. I guess the note worked because Jay, that handsome Native American, asked me out.

I remember our first date like it was yesterday. It was Sunday afternoon, January 18, 1976. He was 21. I was so nervous around him because he was different from anyone I knew. He was quiet and reserved, but I could tell he had a tender heart. We dated on and off for the next four years. I was a Catholic school girl and he was a fascinating bad boy. He said he loved me, but we struggled for years because he couldn't or wouldn't commit, and I didn't understand why.

Then in 1980, life became serious. I was twenty and two months pregnant when he had a serious accident at work, causing the loss of his hand. He withdrew, and I was frustrated that he wasn't there for me like I needed him to be. When our daughter Kelly Jae was born, he tried hard to prove himself as a father, but I thought I knew best how to care for her. I would get upset if he didn't hold her right to soothe her or when he quickly handed her back to me if she fussed. I wondered why Jay was so nervous with our baby and thought parenting should come as naturally for him as it did for me. I assumed that he just didn't love us enough. I was young and didn't know that men parent differently from women but that both ways are right.

After a few months, he asked me to marry him. He said he loved me and that he needed someone who would stand by him and knew he could count on me. This should have been a dream come true, but I said no. I felt he was distracted. He didn't stay focused on Kelly and me like he used to and I felt alone. I didn't feel important to him. I asked him to prove his love by waiting a few years. He must have been crushed. Those years never came and we drifted apart within six months. I loved him so much, but I didn't understand him. It was like we spoke two different languages. So I accepted that we couldn't be together and moved on to raise our daughter alone. He once told me, "You will never forget me because she looks just like me!" And he was right—I couldn't forget him.

Fast Forward Twenty Years

How life can change in an instant! Through a chain of events that only God could have written, our paths crossed again almost twenty years later when my daughter and I unexpectedly ran into Jay's mother at the hair salon. My now adult daughter told me she wanted her grandmother to know who she was, so with awe and joy, I introduced them. As they hugged and cried, I could feel the healing begin. But sadly, his mother told us the news that Jay's father had passed away just three days earlier. As we talked, she also made sure to let me know that Jay had never married. Neither had I. (So I guess we had both waited!)

Two weeks later, Kelly met her father for the first time. As I gazed at the two, I loved that our beautiful daughter, with her proud high cheekbones and stunning features, looked *exactly* like her father. They got acquainted and soon grew to love each other. That day was the start of what would be our new beginning, our do-over, because God's plan was even bigger than we ever could have imagined.

I learned that love has no expiration date. Even when Jay and I both thought it was over, our love quickly found its way back into our lives in a way that was so different from before. Twenty years apart had changed us both. Now I could feel how much he loved us. He still had our prom pictures and all the little gifts I had given him. He showed Kelly her baby pictures, which he'd treasured. I think it was his way of letting her know he had never forgotten us. Jay freely expressed his love for Kelly and me, and I drank it in like the elixir of life. He was strong and masculine and made us feel safe. He wrote beautiful love letters and made me feel like I was the only woman in the world. I was grateful every day for this wonderful man, my first love, who was back in our lives.

But life would challenge us again when Jay lost his mother unexpectedly within a few months. Life became bittersweet. He was grateful for the return of his family but devastated at the loss of his parents. As the months went by and we settled in as a couple, I could feel things starting to get off track. Little things upset him, and our differences started to show and wear on us. Used to being a single mom, I called the shots and ran the show. But instead of admiring this trait, Jay made it clear that he was not going to be controlled by me or anyone else for that matter. He told me he felt disrespected, but I didn't understand why. I felt I was as smart and capable as Jay, so why shouldn't I make decisions for us and show him how to be a good father and husband?

One day at the bank, a teller asked Jay a question and, without thinking, I answered for him like I would answer for a child. Jay snapped that he could answer his own questions. I was so embarrassed that I began to cry, and the teller awkwardly handed me a box of tissues. I imagined that the teller thought I was with a horrible brute, when in reality I was mortified to have treated him like a child in public. No wonder he was mad.

I knew I'd been wrong, so I apologized after we left, but I still didn't know how to change behavior that felt so natural for me. Instead of addressing my controlling issues, I began to question his commitment, as I had before, and the same old insecurities bubbled up. I was scared that the past was going to repeat itself, but I also knew that our love was still strong. I prayed that with God's guidance, I would be shown a new way to make this work. And God, who loves us with creativity and good humor, spoke to me one morning through Katie Couric on *The Today Show*.

Katie's guest was Laura Doyle, author of *The Surrendered Wife*. I listened with amazement as Laura described her marriage as a mirror image of my own relationship, struggles, and feelings. She talked about her ah-ha moment when she realized that she had control issues and that until she could overcome them, she would never be able to be intimate with her husband. I'd had my ah-ha moment at the bank, and I wanted to learn how to change the way I interacted with Jay in the future. So I scribbled the name of her book but hesitated over the title. I was a strong, independent woman—did I really want to *surrender*? But if this was how to bring back my loving, funny man, then the answer was unequivocally yes! I bought the book and found within its pages the magical keys to restore the intimacy with Jay that I missed so much.

The first thing I did was take the quiz "How Intimate Is Your Marriage?" I was relieved to find that we rated high and our relationship was still intimate and passionate! Thankfully we had not had a train wreck yet. There were no brutal fights and threats of breakup, but there were plenty of struggles with our communication. The book outlined how a series of intimacy principles could help me to change my old habits and attitudes to restore the connection in my relationship and help bring out the best in both of us. Laura warned that surrendering is both gratifying and terrifying but yields peace, joy, and feeling good about myself and my marriage. I was all in!

Laura also explained that surrendering doesn't mean giving up my personality or my autonomy. It simply means letting go of unnecessary control and learning to trust my husband. I began to understand that my need to control was caused by underlying fear. I had struggled with trust since my parents' divorce, so surrendering wasn't easy. I soon realized that trust and control issues affected our relationship the first time around and that if I did not address them this time, I could lose my second chance.

Every chapter I read spoke to me, and I was surprised by how quickly I started to see positive results. Respecting Jay became a high priority, so I started listening without trying to change what he was saying or one-up him with my ideas. The invisible "duct tape" that Laura refers to in the book was a constant reminder that I had to allow him to talk and even give him the space to make mistakes without criticism. The better I got at listening, the more he wanted to share with me. The more he shared with me, the more I was impressed with what great ideas he had and how capable he was of taking care of our family.

I had always believed, at least in theory, that the man's role in the household was to lead, and now I understood that I had taken that away from him. This understanding opened the door to trust in our relationship. Because I respected, trusted, and appreciated Jay, it felt safe to let go of control. My fear that things would fall apart was replaced by a comforting feeling of being taken care of by a man who loved me. I spent many years trying to be superwoman and putting on a tough front, but now it was safe to be vulnerable and express my desires. This former tomboy started to feel very feminine in the strong arms of my honey.

The results of surrendering spoke for themselves. By January of the following year, Jay proposed and, of course, this time I said *yes*! We had a beautiful wedding on March 29, 2003, which would have been his parent's fifty-first anniversary. The priest said it was our job to spread hope. Our daughter, now almost twenty-three, stood at the altar. She had surprised Jay the year before by changing her last name to his, so we were finally an official family. Our lives had come full circle.

I continued to work hard at surrendering. The book had become a staple on my nightstand, a well-loved guide that I revisited time and time again. I understood that surrendering was a process and a journey because life was ever changing and old habits die hard! But life felt good, and we were happy. One evening as we were lying in bed, I felt overwhelmed with love. I shared with Jay how grateful I was that I no longer had to carry the load alone. For so many years I had to be strong, but now I could finally relax knowing that he was taking care of our family.

In 2007, life got even better when our grandson, Bryce, was born. Having a grandson brought out a side of Jay that I never got to experience with our daughter and made me fall in love with him all over again. Bryce and "Pop Pop" had a special bond that was beautiful to see.

But wouldn't you know it, having a grandson brought out my old controlling issues again, just like when Kelly was a baby! I secretly believed that I knew more about kids than Jay did and knew the "right" way to do everything. This time Jay made it clear that he didn't need me to teach him how to be a grandfather! And he was right—he was doing a great job. I went back to the basics of surrendering and things got back on track, but I learned a lesson in how new life circumstances could easily throw a monkey wrench in my surrendering.

Our Milestone Anniversary

Over the years, I have told our beautiful love story to perfect strangers over and over again while Jay shook his head and smiled. I would joke that "God brought us back together, but He certainly did not sprinkle fairy dust on us." We worked hard on our marriage, but I know that *The Surrendered Wife* made the difference in our success. The skills I learned there kept my marriage strong and allowed Jay to be a successful husband, father, and grandfather. I was so proud of him. He had more than made up for all of our lost years, and our family was strong.

March was a busy month for us. I was excited to celebrate Jay's fifty-eighth birthday, which would be followed by our tenth wedding anniversary at the end of the month. Kelly, Bryce, Jay, and I celebrated his birthday with our family tradition of homemade spaghetti and meatballs, and a three-layer white cake. We sat at the dining room table eating, laughing, and telling stories while I snapped photos and recorded video, as I usually do. Jay told Bryce it was the best birthday he'd ever had. My surprise for Jay was a "Lobster Gram," which would arrive from Maine in a few days. We decided that he and I would celebrate his birthday again that Saturday evening with a lobster dinner.

Saturday night was everything I imagined. Over delicious lobster, we talked about our upcoming anniversary, we kissed, and we laughed. Love was in the air! I was feeling pretty sexy in my new Victoria's Secret nightgown since it finally fit perfectly (though over the years, Jay never seemed to notice my physical imperfections, and I always felt comfortable and feminine in his arms). As I slipped into bed, I snuggled against him with my Oprah magazine. After a few minutes, he flicked it out of my hands, and it fell to the floor. Surprised, I turned my head to look at him. There he was, smiling that smile and staring at me as if it were the first time he'd seen me. I could feel my heart racing, an effect he still had on me, so I smiled back and said, "You make me just as nervous today as you did when I was sixteen." He said, "Oh, yeah?" then slipped his strong arm around my waist and pulled me to him. "Unforgettable" was our wedding song, and it was still true! Afterward, as I laid my head on his chest, I knew that I was blessed.

Suddenly, I felt Jay's body jerk. I looked up at him and thought, for a moment, that he was teasing me. Then to my horror, I could see that it was real. Jay was having a heart attack, and I knew that our lives would be changed forever.

I called 911 and followed the operator's instructions while begging Jay not to leave us. He stared at me, following my eyes, as if to say he were sorry. I begged God not to take him, but I knew that I was losing him. Kelly and other family members came quickly. Despite our prayers, the paramedics' efforts, and my husband's unbelievable strength, we lost Jay that night. As strong as he was, he didn't have the strength to overcome the heart attack.

Our tenth wedding anniversary was the day we honored Jay with a beautiful memorial service. It was a bittersweet day, full of love and grief. I expressed how grateful I was for our time together and talked about all the things we were going to miss about him. I told our friends and family, "Although there are so many things we're going to miss, we'll never feel a shortage of his love because he gave us enough love in our time together to last us a lifetime."

As time passes and I work through my grief, I have to keep coming back to gratitude. I know that what we had together was special: a once-in-a-lifetime love that not everyone gets to experience. I never question God or ask why. When I cry, it's simply because I miss Jay. I miss his touch, his voice, and his masculine presence that kept our family safe. And when I talk about him, I smile from the inside out because I still feel so blessed.

Surrendering gave me a beautiful gift. I grieve the loss of my husband, but I have no regrets. There was nothing left unsaid and nothing that I wish I had done differently. I loved, honored, and cherished him, just as I'd promised in our vows, but most importantly, I respected him. I allowed Jay to be the man God intended him to be, and in return, he cherished and adored me.

I love you, Jay!

To read more about Darlene and test your Intimacy Skills, visit: http://intimacyandpeace.com/darlene-a-davis/

Chapter 8

The Intervention of Faith

Michelle Edsall

Certified Relationship Coach, Laura Doyle Connect

In the beginning of our twenty-three-year marriage, there was fun, excitement, and a great spark between us, along with two children within the first two and a half years. For the most part, it worked.

Five years into our marriage, my father-in-law passed away, and our world was shaken. I wanted to be there to support my husband. I also wanted to know how he was feeling, how was he grieving, how was he processing the passing of his father. My numerous questions were not well-received, so I became increasingly frustrated that he could not, or would not, express his feelings.

Several months later, we separated for about six months. When we reunited, we went about married life as usual: work, play, running kiddos to and from gymnastics or dance, and whatnot. We had some arguments and were in and out of marriage counseling, moving from counselor to counselor trying to find someone who could help. Things only seemed worse after each session.

At the end of our eighth year of marriage, triplets were born. This added a whole new level of craziness to our lives. Life blurred together for the first few years, and we eventually fell into a routine. Being the efficient, smart, hyperaware, I-can-do-anything mom, I took on many roles. I volunteered outside of the home, started a business, did the yard work and all interior work, grocery shopped, cooked. You name it, I did it, except take out the garbage. That was my husband's job. I joked that someday I would get a superwoman tattoo.

Fast forward to our twentieth year of marriage. We had two children in college and three in middle school. I was tired, resentful, lonely, overwhelmed, and a control freak (though I had no idea, as I just thought I was keeping our life running). I would become irritated by almost anything my husband said or did. I felt he was incompetent, unorganized, unfeeling, and lacked drive. He would spontaneously clean out my car and throw things away, which drove me nuts! Those were my things, my papers; maybe I needed them. Or, he would buy my favorite candy for me just when I had decided I needed to lose a few pounds. He seemed unable to see the dust, dirt, and things out of place around him. He would say, "Just write down for me what you want and I will do it." His response only made me angrier. I would reply with something like, "Are you serious? Can you not look around and see what needs to be done?" Things became so bad that even my husband's breathing would have me on edge. I used to ask him, "Do you need to do that?" and he would respond, "What? Breathe?" and I would respond, "Um, yeah. Don't do it."

I could not stand him any longer. I felt that he was the source of all my pain and that if he left, my life would be glorious. So I again asked him to move out. This time he did not comply so readily. After two and half months of fighting, silent treatments, demands, and threats of divorce, he left. I was so relieved. It seemed the source of all things horrible was gone.

For the first month, I felt like I had space to breathe and the opportunity to finally stop being on edge. The kids were more involved in the day-to-day activities, they helped out more around the house, and life seemed to be okay. I found myself feeling lonely, longing for connection, and being angry that my husband wasn't begging me to take him back. Only a few friends knew my circumstances, as I was embarrassed to be in this situation. My husband would pick up the kids for his visitation time (which I had set up for him because otherwise who knew when the kids would see him), and I would become agitated just seeing him. I longed to have him pursue me, but the very sight of him set me on edge. This ambivalence continued for eight more months. Six months in, I had a phone consultation with a divorce attorney, who said that she was booked solid for three or four more months. I said that was fine and that I could wait, but she suggested I find someone else sooner. As a few more months passed, I became increasingly bitter and resentful, questioning my worth because my husband had not banged my door down trying to win me back. If he loved me, why wasn't he riding in on his white horse and fighting for me? How could he give up so easily? How could he not care?

What I did get was a man who came almost every night to help me give my sick cat IV fluids. This man put his paycheck into the bank every week to support the family and bought little for himself. But even then, I felt those actions were the minimum he owed me. Every night I was angry when he left because he hadn't poked the cat right or it took too many pokes or he wasn't caring enough towards the cat. This cat was my baby. My husband had found him when he was a day old, abandoned, cold, and sickly. I nursed him back to health and, of course, expected my husband to help me nurse him back to health once again. After all, he had given me the cat. After eight and half months of separation, I still could not stand the sight or sound of my husband and felt my only option was divorce. It just made sense to me. I hated him, he seemed to hate me, and I didn't like living in limbo. Enough was enough.

In my van on a sunny day, I decided to call the top divorce lawyer in town. When I asked to make an appointment, the response was not what I expected: "I'm sorry, she is not taking any new clients right now. Would you like a junior lawyer?" "Um, no I want her," I replied. Again, the secretary informed me that she could not take any new clients. I hung up and thought, "That's okay. I'll call the number two lawyer in town; number two is pretty good." So I made the call, expecting to set a date and time to proceed with the divorce. I could not believe what I heard next: "I'm sorry, he is not taking on any new clients at this time. Would you like a junior lawyer?" *What!? No! Seriously?* I quickly apologized, hung up, and threw my phone across the van. I was so mad. I looked up and yelled aloud, "What are you trying to do to me?! I cannot live like this!" I yelled and cried for a bit and then had an amazing idea. I would just tell my husband that he had to file for a divorce.

So that evening after he'd given my sick cat fluids, I told him he had to file for a divorce so we could end this nonsense and move on. He said he would get back to me in a couple days. I wanted to slap him silly. A few days went by and, after coming over to help with the cat once again, he said he did not have peace about filing the papers and did not want to. I was shocked. We didn't like each other, and yet we were not getting a divorce. This was just one more thing that angered me to no end about him. I felt like he was purposefully withholding a divorce to keep me from moving forward.

Throughout this back-and-forth process, I began seeing a counselor. I told her what had happened, what was still happening, and how life was awful, including for my children. My counselor heard all of this and, as usual, she had a book suggestion for me. This time when she told me the title of the book I threw up in my mouth a little. There was no way I was reading anything with the words "surrendered" and "wife" in the title, I thought. She had been living by *The Surrendered Single* book, also by Laura Doyle, for a few years. She shared how it increased respect and connection with the men in her life. I was intrigued but still repulsed by the title. By the time I left, however, my curiosity was piqued, so I drove to the bookstore and found *The Surrendered Wife*.

I read a little right there in the bookstore and decided to buy it. I went home and read it in a day. I was shocked to find myself on almost every page. All the way to the very end, I thought that this woman was secretly gathering information from my life and writing about me. It occurred to me that some of the suggestions I was reading about were probably doable. I thought if what was written in the book was true, then I *might* be able to change a few things. If I could make some changes, then I owed it to my children to try. I also decided I would need to talk to the author and hear firsthand how all of these skills actually worked, so I signed up for one-on-one coaching. I remember those calls with Laura so well. She asked me to do things that, at the time, I thought were crazy, frivolous, and contradictory to who I was.

My first call with her was a bit before Thanksgiving, when I was trying to decide whether to invite my husband or not. I didn't want him there, but the kids did. Laura coached me through inviting him to join us, and I mulled it over after the call. I thought, "Okay. I can just leave a message on his voicemail asking him to Thanksgiving." It was midday, and he almost never answered his cell during the day—the perfect time to call. It rang twice and, suddenly, he answered. I was so dumbfounded that all I could manage was to mumble, "Do you want to come to Thanksgiving?" He responded with a friendly "yes," followed by, "Do you need any help?" In my head, I was screaming *no*! However, I had been coached to say yes to all offers. So I eked out through clenched teeth, "Sure." He then asked if I needed help shopping and I grudgingly replied, "Umm, sure." Then he asked if I needed help with the turkey. I couldn't stand having to say yes to one more thing, so I told him that the turkey had to go in the oven at 3:30 a.m., thinking that he would happily decline. Instead, he asked me if 3 a.m. was a good time to come over to help get it ready. I somehow said something along the lines of, "Yeah, okay," even while my head was screaming, "Are you serious? How on earth could I stand to see him for that long and, in addition, have him help me shop and cook?" I decided I would do what Laura had suggested as well as I could so that on our next coaching call, I could tell her how it hadn't worked. Convinced the holiday would unfold horribly, I was relieved I'd soon be off the hook.

When Thanksgiving came, my husband showed up at that very early hour and was so helpful and friendly. We actually laughed and had a relatively good time (despite my extended family being there). At the end of the day, we were both surprised that we not only managed to spend time together but had fun too. I focused on saying yes, expressing my gratitude, trying to be vulnerable (though I would rather have ripped out my own fingernails), and saying "whatever you think" instead of answering his many, many questions with detailed instructions like I used to. It was all so foreign to both of us, but the results were intriguing. Even though my thoughts were riddled with anxiety—What if he cut the onions too big? Would he remember to peel the carrots before chopping? —I was committed to not letting it come out in my actions.

At my next call, I wasn't able to tell Laura how badly the holiday had failed. Instead, I told her how well it went. To my chagrin, she celebrated this hurdle with me and then challenged me to tell my husband that instead of a divorce, I wanted to reconcile. I remember being speechless over the idea and felt that it was risky and scared the pants off me. She was asking me to give up my safety net. I really didn't want to let go of the very thing that I felt gave me some leverage, but I knew if and when our marriage did fail, I wanted to be able to say I had done everything required and to walk away with a clean conscience.

One night, after helping me again with the cat, he asked if we could have some tea. He made it, and we sat at the kitchen table and made small talk. I was almost sick to my stomach knowing what I needed to say. I took a big breath and looked at the floor— there was no way was I going to look him in the eye—and mumbled just clearly enough that I didn't want a divorce right now and would like to try reconciliation. My heart was beating so fast. He responded by asking what was going on with me, perhaps looking for a clue that he could trust that I was not out to get him. I hemmed and hawed a bit but let him know that I was trying something new. He seemed to like the idea.

Over the next few weeks, I continued learning how to say yes and "whatever you think," how to express my gratitude for things he did for the family and me, and how to do things that brought me happiness. I jumped off the cliff of surrendering and, in the free fall, gave all the financial control to my husband. I received cards, flowers, and jewelry. We went on dates, embraced our newfound connection, and were filled with adoration.

I remember clearly the night my husband said he wanted to move back in. I had been working the principles for about three weeks. We were snuggling and enjoying each other's company when he said, "I want to move back home." I looked him in the eye this time when I told him I would love it if he did. But after a few days had passed and he had not moved his stuff home, I began to press for a day when he would do it. I immediately felt him distance himself from me, but I continued to urge him. After a coaching call, I was able to get back on track and leave it to him to decide when he wanted to move, with no inquiries from me. Within a few days, suddenly his stuff was all moved home.

By the beginning of the new year, we were living a new life. I continued receiving coaching and grew in my resolve to incorporate the principles into my life. The positive results were all the incentive I needed. There was simply no way to deny how the principles changed my life and saved my marriage. It may sound like everything was smooth, which, to a large extent, it was—if I could keep my fears from dictating my decisions. Like the time I was so freaked out about the finances and not knowing what we had that I went to the bank and sat with the safety deposit box. I just needed reassurance we weren't destitute and the safety deposit box and its contents gave me some peace. As I left the bank, my husband saw me and chased me down to the gas station. He came up to my window with a smile on his face, and I rolled my window down. He gave me an enthusiastic "*Hi!*" but I was embarrassed and thought for sure he would confront me about what I was doing. He didn't. He just filled up my van with gas and said it made his day to see me.

Then there was the incident that cemented my husband's trust in the new me. We had driven three hours to pick up our triplets at camp and proceeded to make the drive back, all the while listening to the three of them tell their tales from camp. I was turned sideways in my seat so I could see them and hear all of the talk. Having risen early, I offhandedly said I would love some coffee. Unbeknownst to me, my husband got off at an exit, and I felt the van come to a screeching halt. He was so focused on finding me a coffee shop that he didn't see the red light and almost broadsided another car. The old me would have been screaming at him, telling him how he had almost killed us and how horrible his driving was. Instead, I asked everyone if they were okay, and all responses were yes. Then I said…nothing. My husband pulled into the coffee shop parking lot and asked what I would like. Here is the kicker—I didn't drink coffee anymore. Instead of mentioning this point, I simply told him what I would like and he returned with my latte. I thanked him for my coffee and his thoughtfulness then shared it with the triplets as we drove home.

A few days later, after the kids went to bed, my husband asked if I was going to say something, anything, about what had happened. At first I was confused—say something about what? He said, "You know, the almost accident." Oh yes, that. I told him I really didn't have anything to say. Now it was his turn to be shocked. We sat in silence for a bit and then he responded, "I trusted you before, but with this, I now trust you wholeheartedly." Before, he was always waiting for the other shoe to drop, but after my lack of criticism in response to this incident, something shifted for him that allowed a much deeper trust in me. Trust that this new way was here to stay. I got to decide that day how I was going to respond, and it was a pretty easy choice knowing he was only trying to make me happy.

Around this time, I knew I wanted to help other women renew their relationships and bring them back from the brink of death. I decided to enroll in Laura Doyle's Relationship Coach Training, not fully realizing how much of an impact it would make in my life. I studied the principles in more depth and put them into practice daily, building one upon another. I still had some areas to work on though. For example, saying "ouch" and "I'm sorry I was disrespectful" were two areas I had a difficult time with, but through the training program, I saw some amazing growth. About the third time I apologized to my husband for being disrespectful, he just told me it was okay. Each apology I offered turned the situation back toward our connection with each other, further cementing our new, more intimate relationship.

I am so excited and grateful to be part of the team of Laura Doyle Certified Intimacy Coaches, a network of amazing women who understand firsthand what it's like to turn a struggling relationship into a thriving one. Now I get to help other women do the same. I love coaching, watching the rebirth of relationships, and sharing with other women all that I have learned to help them create lasting intimacy in their lives.

To read more about Michelle and test your Intimacy Skills, visit: http://intimacyandpeace.com/michelle-edsall/

Chapter 9

Mastering Intimacy and Motherhood

Courtney Elder
Certified Relationship Coach, Laura Doyle Connect

My husband, Thomas, is the perfect man for me. I believe that now, and I believed that when we married, but during the in-between period I wasn't always so sure. We met when I was twenty-one, were engaged four months later, and married just before my twenty-third birthday. I thought he was the most amazing man I could've ended up with: smart, funny, and marching to the beat of his own drum. I was so in love that I overlooked his little imperfections and thought we would be blissfully happy forever.

What I didn't realize then was that real life happens. One month before our first wedding anniversary, we found out I was expecting. Due to our own stupid decisions, we filed for bankruptcy while I was pregnant, and to "start over" we moved 600 miles away when our son was only three months old. The stress of our financial state combined with being a new mom started shining a light on all those "little imperfections." My husband was a stay-at-home dad while I worked outside of the home. I often found myself coming home to a mess or calling him in the middle of the day to find he was engrossed in the newest Xbox game. I was so frustrated and judgmental; I felt that I had *two* children to look after! My husband was this man-child who wasn't living up to the expectations I had for him as a stay-at-home parent.

All our fights didn't seem to be getting my message across that he needed to change, so my next tactic was to force him into doing what I wanted him to. One morning I left for work with the Xbox controllers in the trunk of my car. I figured I would come home to a clean house and have the life I envisioned. Instead, I came home to a messy house and a husband who seemed like he didn't want to be there. My passive aggressive actions didn't change my husband; they only caused us to fight more and take away our intimacy. I vividly remember fighting over the phone while I was at work and being so mad that I would take off my wedding ring and not wear it for the day. I complained to coworkers and girlfriends about Thomas all the time. No wonder none of my friends liked him—I was only sharing his negative traits!

Yet beneath the struggling and fighting, I had a deep love for my husband. In 2010, though still financially stressed, we decided to have another child. By the time our second son was born in 2011, we had settled into what I thought was a pretty normal marital groove. We fought somewhat regularly, and since we both have tempers, our fights would last a few hours with yelling and slamming doors. My parents fought this way, so I thought that was just how married people fought. Never did the words *respect* or *acknowledgement* come to mind. I was still bent on my view that my husband wasn't doing enough around the house and that I was the one doing all the work. It was so tiring having to work forty hours a week then come home and clean, take care of the kids, and try to wrangle my husband's spending into the mold I prescribed.

I had no concept of what self-care was. Not only was I more and more resentful toward my husband but I started taking my frustration out on the kids as well. I felt my boys were such bad children, and I was frustrated whenever they asked me something or didn't follow directions instantly. During my more frustrating moments, I thought, "I work all week and now you want me to do more?" This was the silent complaint raging through my head most nights and weekends.

By this point, I think Thomas was sick and tired of how I was treating him. He would hang out at friends' houses at least three or four nights a week. Looking back, I don't blame him one bit—I was so controlling and degrading toward our entire family that I sympathize with his wanting to get out. But, of course, at the time, I turned his outings into more fuel to feed my fire of "He gets to have all the fun and I have to do all the work." I built up so much resentment that I made up my mind I had chosen the wrong guy and didn't want to be married to him anymore.

In February 2014, my mother-in-law came to visit us. She and I have a great relationship, as if she were my birth mother. One night the three of us were sitting around talking, and we touched on some emotional topics. I remember crying and admitting to them that I was so resentful toward the boys that I wished Thomas and I hadn't had children. We talked for a long time that night about my frustration with life in general, and it was obvious to me that I needed help. I had gone to counseling several times on and off during my adult life but had never found the key to just being happy. I knew it was time for a change.

When I reached out to my mother-in-law, her first suggestion was to reread *The Surrendered Wife*, which she had given me before my wedding. When I read it the first time, I brushed it off, not thinking it was anything that could help me. This second time, it blew my socks off. I felt like Laura and I were the same person. All of the struggles and complaints she had were nearly identical to my own! I realized this book was the key to having a happy life. I reached out to get one-on-one coaching from one of Laura's coaches and began my transformation.

My transformation was challenged only a few days after surrendering. For some reason, we weren't getting our mail, and we were expecting important things, such as paychecks and bills, that we couldn't afford to be lost. The post office hours didn't jive with my work schedule, so I asked Thomas if he could sort it out. Error number one was asking him to do it instead of expressing a pure desire for help. Nonetheless, my wonderful husband said he would take care of it. A few days went by and we still hadn't gotten mail, so I assumed he hadn't called anyone and was being lazy about the whole thing.

When I confronted him (yet another mistake) it turned into a fight. I was so distraught that our mail wasn't being delivered and lamented about why he couldn't just make one phone call to resolve it! In his wisdom he said to me, "Just because you said you can't do it doesn't mean I automatically will." That was a turning point for me. Surrendering isn't about being manipulative so that my husband will do what I want; it's about being vulnerable and trusting that he wants to take care of me and has my best interests at heart. It's about having faith that if he doesn't call the post office, the world won't end.

It turns out he *had* taken care of it. He had kept his eye out for the mail carrier and spoken with her directly, taking care of the whole problem in his own way and in his own time. From that initial failure to implement the principles, I grew so much and tackled future situations in a more respectful and surrendered way.

However, it didn't come without challenges. Just because I had read *The Surrendered Wife* didn't mean that all of our problems went away. We still fought, but now Thomas would hand me my phone and suggest that I call my coach. I remember several times sitting on the sidewalk crying, telling my coach how I thought Thomas was wrong and that he wouldn't do this or didn't do that. I was always asked the same thing: Whose paper was I on? I think that was one of the biggest and most impactful concepts that fueled my transformation. When I got married, I assumed that *everything* about us became one so I could tell my husband what to do because there was no distinction between us. I failed to realize that we were still two distinct people who have different opinions, different thought processes, and different ways of handling emotions. Once I recognized that some things were mine to work through and some were his, I was able to get off his back and stop acting like I was his boss.

I went through private coaching for several months and saw some amazing changes. My husband would compliment me regularly on how much growth he was seeing in me. We were a happier couple. My kids made me happier, and I found myself bragging about how cute they were instead of complaining about how annoying they were. Thomas started going out of his way to do things for me, including little things like put the kids to bed without discussing it or buying my favorite ice cream. It was remarkable to see, after so much time and money wasted at therapy, that *The Surrendered Wife* was the one thing that changed everything.

The biggest change that came about for me was when my husband took over the finances. We were having an argument one day about our bills and how broke we constantly were. I was always so stressed out about handling our money. I felt like we never had enough and the strain of trying to make everything work was a constant. I was distraught during this particular disagreement, and out of the blue Thomas said that he was taking over our finances. He didn't really give me a choice; he just told me that's the way it was going to be. I was so afraid! We had discussed this very thing years ago, and his philosophy on bills was, "If I have the money I'll pay them; if I don't have the money I won't."

I had a strange mixture of fear and relief when he took the responsibility off my shoulders. I couldn't stand to think about what might happen if he skipped a payment, but at the same time I had a deep inner trust in him and was thankful that he was going to be handling the money from now on. Pretty soon after he started taking care of our finances, I found that I was spoiled with gifts much more often and even had an allowance to spend on whatever I wanted. My husband transformed into such a mastermind with our money that two amazing things happened: He left his job for a lower-paying but more satisfying one, and seven months later we bought our first house!

I continued receiving coaching, and after a few months, my coach made an offer that terrified me. She let me know that in a few weeks, Laura was starting a class to train women how to become coaches themselves. I told her that I was just barely getting comfortable with the skills myself and that I couldn't envision myself helping others just yet. She let me think about it and told me that this opportunity may not present itself again so I should really consider it. I knew she was right. I had to get over my fear of not being good enough and not doing things perfectly, so I enrolled in Laura's June 2014 Coach Training Program. It was unlike anything I had expected—the group of women who attended our weekly calls were just like me! We all had the same struggles and were trying to make changes using the same set of Intimacy Skills.

I had homework every week and the opportunity to communicate with these gals and look to them for support. It gave me great joy to support them as well when they were having a trying time. The Coach Training Program, including the repetition of practicing The Six Intimacy Skills, made a huge difference in my transformation. It was like a jet pack taking me to a new level of comfort and ease; no longer did I have to stop and formulate my words carefully to make sure I was saying the right thing. The more I practiced the skills with the women in my coaching group, the more comfortable I was with my husband. For the last part of the class, we were asked to get a practice client and to have coaching calls with her.

One of my closest girlfriends was going through a difficult time with her husband, so she agreed to let me practice coaching with her. I vividly remember after one of our calls I had the strangest mix of emotions that I had never experienced before. I was almost brought to tears because I was so sad that I once had a marriage in such turmoil. Her challenges were the exact same ones I was facing only one year earlier. I felt ashamed for treating my husband the way I had and for letting our relationship get so bad. But when I was speaking to my friend on the phone, I also felt so much joy and hope that her marriage could be everything she wanted it to be. I explained that I was absolutely amazed at how good things were now and that she could have that for herself too.

At the end of the class, we were given the choice to become a coach. I experienced such a life-changing shift that I knew I had to take advantage of the opportunity to help others. In December 2014, I became a Laura Doyle Certified Relationship Coach. That's not to say, however, that I am a Surrendered Wife one hundred percent of the time. I wish I were, but since I'm human, I make mistakes too.

My goal is to reach other young moms, whether they work outside of the home or within. I want them to see how changing the dynamic of their marriages can change their entire family life. We have a happier home now because I treat my husband with dignity and respect. He truly is my equal partner in life. The process of being a Surrendered Wife is ongoing, and I hope to learn and grow every day. I have wonderful women around me who support me, and I strive to be a resource for those who are in need.

To read more about Courtney and test your Intimacy Skills, visit: http://intimacyandpeace.com/courtney-elder/

Chapter 10

Learning How to Love Again

Sarah Ellis

Certified Relationship Coach, Laura Doyle Connect

It's hard for me to revisit the miserable place that I was in four years ago. I was hopeless and terribly sad. My thoughts revolved around divorce and how I could not continue living the way I was living. I was desperate; I bounced from one therapist to another. My husband and I were full of resentment towards each other, and everything he did was wrong in my eyes. He had already shared with me that he didn't like my company. He was always leaving and wasn't home often.

I thought he just didn't love or care about me. There was a lot of drama in my life, and I was constantly feeling hurt. I didn't feel like he heard me or considered what I wanted. I kept trying to explain to him how disappointed I was and, for some reason, he continued to withdraw from me. He became cold and unavailable when I was sad and hurt. I was lonely and, as time went on, I grew hopeless, thinking that my husband was not capable of providing me with emotional support.

Things hadn't always been that way. When I married him, he was interesting and had a great sense of humor. His knowledge and sharp mind never ceased to amaze me and he was so kindhearted. He was head over heels, wrote me love letters, and couldn't do enough to make me happy. We were blissful.

I was determined to have a great marriage after seeing my parents fail in theirs, but I had no idea *how* to make a good marriage. When things were good and there was no stress, we were friends. But as soon as any conflict or even a difference of opinion came up, we turned into enemies. I became a martyr. I didn't share my true feelings or desires, and I went along with everything he did until I just couldn't take it anymore and erupted. I started showing my disapproval of him and criticizing what he did. I started trying to control him, desperate for things to go my way. I became critical and unhappy, and my husband became distant and cold. Slowly, there were less and less of the good times, and then, about four years ago, I hit rock bottom.

I kept trying therapy, thinking that someone had a solution to my marital unhappiness. One therapist told me that I should consider my options (like divorce), and another listened to my soliloquy of negativity and agreed with it all, indicating that my husband needed to change or we were doomed. Another therapist told me I couldn't say anything negative for the next five years. I couldn't tell him anything that hurt, bothered me, or made me sad for five years—as if that were realistic! Another told me always to be calm, without offering any advice on how to achieve that.

I knew that things could be different because about two years into my marriage a friend introduced me to Laura Doyle's book *The Surrendered Wife*. She came to visit right after my husband and I had had a fight. She took one look at me and asked what had happened. She proceeded to tell me how following Laura Doyle's principles in *The Surrendered Wife* saved her marriage. I was intrigued. She gave me the book, and I read it in one sitting. It actually helped me a lot.

I began practicing gratitude, and the atmosphere in our home changed. My husband basked in all the appreciation he was receiving from his new, gracious wife. I became aware of the ways I was controlling him and of subtle behaviors that were disrespectful towards him and our marriage. Things improved—as long as I was in a good mood, healthy, and strong. As soon as I became needy and vulnerable or there was stress in our lives, the atmosphere reverted to the way things had been.

We had just relocated across the continent, things were extremely stressful, and my husband and I were growing further and further apart. One day, I decided to Google "Laura Doyle" in the hope of finding support. I knew that the only thing that was somewhat working for me in my relationship were the principles in her book. I was starving for love, compliments, and emotional support, and even though it is common for couples to argue from time to time, I couldn't figure out why stressful situations caused such a deep divide between us. I simply could not understand why my husband didn't want to be there for me when I needed emotional support. I thought if anyone could help me, it would be Laura.

I enrolled in Laura's Coach Training Program and loved it. I had so many ah-ha moments, and the mysteries of my relationship began to unravel before my eyes. I realized that I was rejecting my husband because of an image of how he was *supposed* to look, behave, and speak. When he attempted to be there for me, I didn't appreciate it and tried to control how he supported me, as if I could dictate that. I was comparing him to the other men in my life, expecting him to be like my brothers and father. Most of all, I wanted him to be more like me!

When I learned to accept him and respect him for who he is, to be open to the way he does things, and to receive his emotional support graciously (even if he wasn't as romantic or empathetic as I wanted him to be) he began to feel safe to be himself. He started really hearing and listening to me. I will never forget the first time he apologized to me, which was an awesome breakthrough! He began taking more responsibility for his actions, and he no longer needed to be defensive because there was no more criticism and control coming from me. I learned what it meant to truly trust and respect my husband as a man and as an individual.

Even though I experienced many wonderful breakthroughs in the coach training, I still had setbacks. I often made demands and requests of my husband instead of sharing my feelings. I was subtly controlling, and my body language sent a clear message that I did not approve of him in many ways. When he tried to be there for me, he wasn't doing it the way I thought he should and was always disappointing me.

My husband is a brilliant, intellectual guy, but he just does not like feelings. I could not understand why he wasn't taking the opportunities I was "giving" him to express how happy he was with me. (Duh! Maybe he wasn't all that happy!) I put so much pressure on him based on the assumption that he should act according to the predetermined scenario that was playing in my head. So my husband grew frustrated that he could never do anything right and could never meet my unspoken expectations.

I remember when I was going through the training, our washing machine broke. I had supper waiting on the table, and I was starving. My husband went down to try and fix it. After playing with it for a few minutes, he realized it was really broken. He started bailing out the water in the tub with an empty detergent can that had a spout, which was taking forever. I wanted to tell him that this was futile, that he would be at it all night, and that supper was getting cold. I started to tell him that I didn't think that way was a good idea, but I stopped in mid sentence, closed my mouth, and, as Laura puts it, "stayed on my own paper." I realized that what I really wanted was to eat. So I said, "I want to eat!" He then looked up at me and said, "Okay, let's go" and told me that he probably should use a bigger bucket to empty the machine anyway. Can you believe it?! He came to the same conclusion as me all by himself, *and* we were able to enjoy each other's company over dinner. Maybe he just liked figuring things out on his own.

I used to feel my husband was wrong from a parenting point of view all the time. He would bring home junk food and sugary cereal that I didn't approve of. He would sometimes play roughly with the kids or throw the baby up in the air too high or after a meal. Now I know how to trust in my husband's abilities as a father, even if his parenting varies from mine. I just tell myself that he is their father and loves them very much so he would never do anything unsafe or cause them harm. When I look around for evidence of this, I see it all the time. He has never hurt them. My children love that he is so much fun, and I have come to accept that

I'm the stricter parent. He has also taught me to let go sometimes too.

I recognize that both parents will have distinctly different parenting methods and that giving my husband space to be the father he wants to be is crucial for our relationship and for my kids. Now, he has free rein to do whatever he wants with them, to spoil them, to give them whatever suits his fancy (even if that means feeding them sugary cereal right before lunch!). I am with the kids most of the time, so I parent them the way I want to. It took a lot of letting go, but I'm grateful to have a husband who is creating wonderful memories for kids who adore him.

Perhaps one of the hardest aspects of the training was figuring out how to take care of myself. When I was growing up, I had the "want" trained out of me. I considered only what I had to do or should do. Since my early years, I've had a hard time making myself a priority. I struggled with putting my needs before everything that had to get done and everyone who needed me. What I learned about self-care is that my happiness is *only* my responsibility. When I'm not needy or desperate, I exude serenity and contentment, which makes me more attractive. People don't want to give to those who will drain them and never be satisfied. People do want to give to those who are receptive and gracious and whose needs are met. That's the type of person I want to be: one who shows others how I want to be treated by the way I treat myself.

Once, when I was worn down from a lingering cold, my brother called to let me know that he was coming over and that he needed me to give him a ride to an appointment. My house needed to be cleaned, my kids were home, and I was having company for dinner. When he walked in, he decided that he also needed lunch. As you can imagine, my patience was wearing thin. I showed him to the fridge, and he went digging. At that point, I realized that everyone had better stay out of my path because I knew I was not going to be nice. I had planned on making another dish for dinner that night, but instead I left everyone and everything to take a forty-five-minute nap. When I got up from my nap, I felt so refreshed. I even thanked my husband for taking over while I napped. He loved having his calm, rested wife around, and we had plenty enough food for dinner that evening. I know that it is *my responsibility* to take care of myself and that when I fulfill this responsibility, everyone around me benefits from my good mood.

I began to truly own my happiness. I finally realized my value as a person and started taking better care of myself. I did everything I could to make sure that I was happy, calm, and relaxed. I became more attuned to the stressors that put me over the edge, and I let go of some of my unrealistic expectations of how I thought my life should look. My relationship with my husband now takes priority over a clean house. I learned that resentment is toxic to our relationship, so if I felt something would make me resentful, I avoided it and learned to say "I can't" instead. I learned to go to a place of vulnerability and to expose my pain instead of getting angry. I began to express my desires purely, without being attached to the outcome. To my surprise, as I began getting better at the skills, I also began receiving all sorts of small gifts, which I now treasure. We were in love again.

I am proof that surrendering works. I no longer have the struggles I use to have. I truly respect and trust my husband. I have no more resentment. I am vulnerable when I'm sad or upset. My husband is attuned to me. He listens to me, takes good care of me, and is always trying to please me. He is caring and is there for me.

Today, I live my dreams. I have a good, solid marriage, and the ups and downs of life actually bring us closer, whereas in the past they pushed us farther apart. We enjoy each other's company and support one another.

My husband is present for me in ways I never imagined he would be. One of my coworkers asked what my secret is, why my husband calls me a few times a day to check in with me and inquire about my wellbeing, when her husband of twenty years doesn't.

My secret is being vulnerable. My secret is expressing my desire and letting go of control. My secret is taking care of myself and practicing gratitude for my husband and all he does for me.

I now know what true love is and how to keep it alive.

To read more about Sarah and test your Intimacy Skills, visit: http://intimacyandpeace.com/sarah-ellis/

Chapter 11

The Power of Kindness

Jineen Glover

Certified Relationship Coach, Laura Doyle Connect

I grew up in a home where we talked openly about relationships. My dad was a marriage and family counselor, so I heard a lot of conversations about how to have a successful marriage. Despite my father's training and counsel, my parents struggled to understand each other and have peace in their relationship, and I ended up bringing the same things to my own marriage.

The first year or so of my marriage was lonely. I was living in a town without any friends or family. My husband's large family lived in the same town but didn't know me well, and I felt misunderstood by them. It was difficult for me. I felt like my husband never understood me either and we were emotionally disconnected. I soon got pregnant, which we were excited about, but we didn't realize how adding kids to the situation would present even more challenges to our communication and intimacy. I always longed for more quality time with my husband, craving an emotional connection in order for him to understand me better.

I discovered *The Surrendered Wife* while raising small children and just trying to physically survive. I was drawn to the unique title of the book and, of course, Laura's vulnerability in sharing her own story. I loved what I read but wasn't ready or able to apply the principles. It wasn't until several years later, when I entered into Laura's Coach Training Program, that I decided to really surrender. Though my marriage was okay, I felt it was lacking in intimacy, peace, emotional connection, and affection. I kept wanting to feel closer and more connected to my husband but struggled to make it happen.

One of the biggest struggles in my relationship before learning the Intimacy Skills was how I communicated. When I started hearing my tone and how I was not speaking to my husband respectfully, it was upsetting to see the hurt I was causing. Having heard this kind of communication growing up, I had a hard time realizing that it was actually doing more damage than good. My husband is one of the kindest people I know, and he couldn't understand why I wasn't kind in return when I spoke to him. I found that when I spoke disrespectfully, he automatically shut down. Eventually, I learned how to ask things nicely instead of demanding them, speaking in a softer, more feminine way. Simply showing him respect started making such a difference in our relationship.

It can be hard surrendering when switching gears from mom to wife. Like most mothers of young children, I was in charge of it all. But there is a huge difference in the way you speak to a child compared to your husband. He is not a child—he's a grown man who doesn't need to be told what to do or how to do it. Avoiding instructing him, however, was easier said than done. Although deep down I hated speaking to my husband as if I were his mother, I simply didn't know how to address him any other way. What I realized through the training is that this was not only demeaning and disrespectful but also humiliating to him.

I hate to admit how many times I felt the need to tell him what to do and how and when to do it, like I knew better than him. I used to just want him to do things the way I thought they should be done, which I now know is so controlling! Once I realized that I could, and should, let go of my controlling behavior and allow my husband the opportunity to do things his way, it made a big impact on our relationship. At first, it was difficult because I was afraid that my life would fall apart and that nothing would ever get done or, if it did get done, it wouldn't be my way and I'd just have to do it over. I soon found it was far more rewarding to have peace, intimacy, and a passionate relationship with my husband, who loved me and wanted to make me happy, rather than being right and trying to control everything!

But these rewards also came with a big helping of humility. When I started this practice, part of what showed up for me was how much I needed to apologize for my disrespectful ways. At first, I really hated having to say that I was sorry for being rude or sarcastic or disrespectful. Swallowing my pride and telling my husband that I was wrong and that I was sorry took some time getting used to. Who loves to admit they're wrong? But when I came across as demanding or blaming, listed all of the things he hadn't done, or spoke to him disrespectfully, it would bring him down physically and emotionally, leaving him with no desire to be anywhere near me. While learning how to apologize may not have been easy, it has made such a difference in our relationship because my husband doesn't feel like a target for my attacks and criticism. Instead, he feels heard and respected, and he has the freedom to be himself without the fear of repercussion from me.

Since surrendering, I have learned how to stay on my side of the street, so to speak, and not focus on his shortcomings. I know now that I can change only my behavior; I am responsible for me and what I do in our relationship, but I am not in charge of him or how he behaves. Once again, it is a reminder that I am not his mother, and I certainly don't want to be!

The difference that I see in my husband since I've been a Surrendered Wife is pretty great! He seems less stressed; he doesn't seem like he's carrying the weight of the world on his shoulders. We laugh and enjoy each other's company so much more. He doesn't feel like I'm always on his case, and I can tell he feels more like the man God created him to be! I can't believe how many burdens we lift off of our husbands when we relinquish control, get off of their backs, and let them be men! Not only do they feel better about themselves, but they are even sexier to us when we see them be who they were created to be.

A few years ago, when I was just starting to surrender, my husband and I went through a difficult time with our finances. He had acquired some money, but instead of being open with me about it, he was deceitful. Because I was hurt by his actions, we decided that I should handle the family's finances for a while. We had taken turns with them prior to this, but this time it definitely seemed like I should be handling them. But after a few years, I realized that in order to be fully surrendered, I needed to hand the finances back over to him. This was huge for me because I was telling him that I fully trusted him again. Relinquishing control of our finances was so empowering for him! It was as if I had given him permission to take care of us the way he saw fit and that I was okay with the outcome, whatever it may be. Not long after I let go of the finances, he left his six-figure income to pursue his dream career, something I'm not sure he ever would have done if I hadn't completely trusted him with them.

Surrendering seems to impact every aspect of my life. If I learn to let go of control, my husband steps up to be the man he wants to be for me. When I relinquished the finances, he blew me away with his ambition, drive, and generosity. He made more money and was full of motivation. In her book, Laura says that when you relinquish control of your finances, you will likely see more gifts, which is surprisingly true!

I am disappointed to say that, initially, I was not an easy one to win over when it comes to gifts. My husband sometimes went out of his way to buy me a gift that wasn't something I liked, and I said so. Once, he bought me some perfume that I had never smelled before and really didn't like. I told him so and, of course, this made him feel terrible. What was the point of that? Not only did it make me seem ungrateful but it didn't benefit our relationship at all; in fact, it made him never want to get me anything again! This is where being grateful and saying "thank you" are so important! Everyone wants to feel appreciated for going out of his way for someone. It makes him feel good that he can take care of you, help you, or just bring a smile to your face. I still struggle sometimes with receiving from my husband, especially if he gives me something that I wouldn't have picked out myself, but the gesture simply means he is thinking of me, and I find it so sweet that he goes out of his way to make me happy!

One day, while I was doing some self-care and taking a bath, I was blown away by my husband's attentiveness. Before surrendering, my husband used to listen to me talk, but I sometimes felt like he didn't care because he was distracted or not paying much attention. On this day, however, he came over to the tub, knelt down, and looked into my eyes as I shared with him my day. That is when I realized these principles were working!

So many times in the past, I wished my husband would do something thoughtful and romantic. Now it seems like he is more romantic and sweet than I ever gave him credit for! Not long ago, I was at church early to lead worship for Sunday service, when my husband showed up with my favorite coffee and donut. Again, I was blown away that he had gone out of his way to bring me something he knows I love, and I felt so special and taken care of!

The minute I seem to think I have this Surrendered Wife thing down, I realize I don't, and I end up rereading or listening to Laura's book. For example, I found myself complaining to my husband last night about something I asked him to get me from the store. I didn't handle it well and, while I'd like to blame PMS for my less-than-stellar behavior, I know better! What I should've done was just say thank you for getting me what I wanted, even if it wasn't exactly how I wanted it. But instead, my husband felt attacked, which ruined the night. It was another reminder that I may not always get it right, but when I do try to keep an open mind and heart, it's so much better for both of us.

I continue to work on being relaxed and not feeling the need to control, but every so often, fear creeps in. That's when I start feeling the need to control the strongest. The reality is that control is an illusion based on fear. When I do feel the urge, I know it's my cue to focus on taking care of myself, to remind myself to stay on my own paper, and to trust in my husband. What has been really eye-opening is recognizing my own controlling behavior in one of my daughters. One day, I heard her telling her father what to do and was blown away. I realized that not only does she have a very strong personality but she must have seen me model this bossy behavior. I had to address the issue immediately and help her understand that she wasn't respecting her father and that this was not how she should be talking to any man! I've noticed this same kind of interaction between my son and daughter as well, and he does not respond positively to being told what to do and being disrespected. I am amazed that, no matter the age, boys and men are just programmed to desire respect.

I am definitely different from the wife I used to be—thank God! I have learned I don't always have to be right and or have the last word. My husband is very smart, smarter than me most of the time, so I don't have to tell him how to do things. I've learned that respect is key for a man and that kindness spoken makes a world of difference. Being thankful to someone for even the smallest gesture makes him feel appreciated, and saying thank you is so important. Relinquishing control is not as scary as you think—once you actually do it! It's actually very freeing and has taken many burdens off of my shoulders. It's amazing how we think claiming all control keeps everything steady and moving, when really it's just the opposite. It actually makes me feel more stressed and overwhelmed, while relinquishing control gives me space to breathe, relax, and enjoy life.

It is still unbelievable to me that when I am kind and respectful towards my husband and am vulnerable with him, we have so much peace, love, and quality time together. Not only is he way more attentive, thoughtful, and affectionate towards me but he also gets much more done for me around the house, which is a huge bonus! He constantly shows me his love and strives to make me happy. When I truly live the principles, it is so clear that he *wants* to make me happy!

Without *The Surrendered Wife*, I believe my marriage would be stressful and lonely, lacking the peace and intimacy that we have now. I encourage other women to read *The Surrendered Wife* because it will change your marriage if you allow it to! Women really do hold all the power in relationships, and men love to see us embrace our softer, more feminine side! It is a never-ending journey but so much sweeter since learning to live surrendered!

To read more about Jineen and test your Intimacy Skills, visit: http://intimacyandpeace.com/jineen-glover/

Chapter 12

An Education in Love

Cheryl Johnson
Certified Relationship Coach, Laura Doyle Connect

I've done a lot of work around my personal issues. I have lots of them, given that my mother had schizophrenia in my formative years. I'm talking about years of personal therapy, dozens of hours of Erhard Seminars Training, and ten years of college classes, mostly in psychology. I wanted to understand what had happened to my mother and to our family. It was a long and painful process, but I finally realized that whatever had happened, I couldn't blame my mother for the shape my life was in. She was the victim of a horrible mental disease. So if I couldn't blame her any more, then I had to be responsible for the choices I made and the life I had created. That was a hard pill to swallow.

Interestingly, throughout all of that personal growth, my relationships remained a mess. I married the first time for all the wrong reasons and blamed that husband for not being present or mentally available for me. So after nine years, I asked for a divorce. I married again a couple of years later, thinking that I could make my new guy better. That didn't work. He was not a good guy. We all know we can't change anyone but ourselves, right? Apparently, I thought I was exempt from that principle, and after eleven years of marriage and countless attempts to change him, I left him.

All I truly wanted was safety and security, but it seemed that even after all of my hard work, I couldn't make that happen. I always blamed someone or something else and found myself alone. As I grew older and more educated, I still felt like a complete failure with my romantic relationships. So I remained single, dated through social websites, and hoped for the best. After putting myself through school and completing my master's degree in counseling, I found comfort in knowing that I had a great career and could take care of myself.

Then, three years ago, I met the man of my dreams. Mike and I get along great, make each other laugh, thoroughly enjoy each other's company, and my friends and family always comment on how happy we look. He's such an easygoing guy, so steady, sensible, and really fun. He provides the security I've been seeking for so long. We are truly great together.

So, nothing was wrong with our relationship, and we could've continued fine this way, except one day, my friend recommended a book entitled *The Surrendered Wife*. This book made me think about things I normally wouldn't spend much time thinking about and had never specifically worked on. I began putting into practice the skills of intimacy and vulnerability: being respectful and grateful, taking care of myself, and being more feminine when I'm at home versus when I'm at work. These skills made total sense to me and seemed to complement all the work that I'd done in my extensive counseling training. The skills I learned help me to choose intimacy consciously rather than trying to control or manipulate situations unconsciously. Becoming more aware of these concepts added even more depth and meaning to my relationship with Mike.

One of the biggest benefits of practicing the Intimacy Skills has been learning to express myself to Mike without being attached to the outcome or making him wrong for not doing what I think he should do. I knew early on that I wanted to marry Mike, but he felt that he would never get married again. I had resigned myself to the unhappy fact that I would either have to live with Mike's decision and never be married again or have to leave him and find a man willing to commit to marriage. Neither of these choices was acceptable. I loved Mike and certainly did not want to leave him. I knew that much, but I also knew that I had to be honest and express my desire.

After reading Laura's book and thinking more about what I really wanted (that ever-elusive security), Mike and I had a beautiful and intimate conversation one evening. I shared my desire to be married. I simply expressed my desire authentically and without any attachment by stating, "I'm the marrying kind. I really need and want to be married. I can't change that. It's just me." I also let him know that I understood and respected his choice to remain unmarried. I literally had no expectation; I just wanted to be clear and honest with him. I had no idea what would happen. I was more than a little terrified to be so vulnerable, and I did not want either of us to deal with a poor result.

His response blew me away. He confided that lately he had been thinking a lot about marrying me. He said he didn't want to lose me because of things that had happened in his past and he was struggling to resolve what he needed to before taking the next step. He said he would do whatever it took to marry me. An impromptu sort of proposal followed, and incredibly, that very evening, we began planning our wedding!

I learned a lot from this interaction. I had been operating out of the fear of loss and abandonment, but as soon as I allowed myself to be really open and vulnerable with the man I loved, something incredible happened. As amazing as it was, getting what I wanted wasn't the point. The truly incredible part was that I felt relieved and safe. It felt good to be vulnerable and feminine and simply myself with Mike. I learned that he can take care of me only if I tell him what I need and want honestly and respectfully.

There's something in Laura Doyle's work that's available to every woman who's interested in having a wonderful, close relationship with her husband or rediscovering the man of her dreams. That in itself is pretty great, but there are also some side benefits. First, I have a husband I love and respect so much, who gives me everything I ever dreamed of! I feel better and more confident as I practice taking care of myself. I understand that I don't need to have the same intensity and drive at home that I do at work. My husband takes care of our money, and I don't have to think twice about it. I am so grateful every day for all that life has to offer.

These are some of the reasons why I became a Laura Doyle Relationship Coach. Laura describes this surrendered state as being "cherished and adored for life." I think we all deserve that kind of love, and coaching other women through this work is one way I can share the skills while keeping them alive in my own life every day. I invite all my women friends to take a chance on these skills. You don't know what might be around the corner—I didn't either.

To read more about Cheryl and test your Intimacy Skills, visit: http://intimacyandpeace.com/cheryl-johnson/

Chapter 13

A Second Chance at Respect

Julie Koehn

Certified Relationship Coach, Laura Doyle Connect

After a messy divorce and almost ten years as a single parent, I met Frank. I was always guarded about dating while raising my daughter. However, I realized that Frank was different. I came to find out that he was, in fact, one of the good guys. We were introduced at church. Knowing that we both believed in God was important to both of us. We needed the Holy Spirit to guide us if we were heading towards marriage again.

I was twelve years into our marriage when a new friend, Elaine, asked me to read *The Surrendered Wife*. I was willing to read it for two reasons: I trusted this woman because I thought she had a great thirty-plus-year marriage, and I had already spent the past five years digging deeper into what makes a good marriage. I wanted a closer relationship with my husband, which I hadn't achieved yet.

I struggled with the title at first. I assumed "surrendering" was more about submitting to my husband's leadership, whether I liked it or not. That did not sit well with me because I assumed it meant I had to give up my identity. But, I did read on. The subtitle read, "A Practical Guide For Finding Intimacy, Passion, and Peace With a Man." Now, that caught my attention! From that point until the last page of the book, I held onto every word and found myself excited and hopeful about practicing what Laura was teaching.

I was determined that this marriage would be perfect and last a lifetime. The engagement had been short and very sweet. It was the day before the wedding that we had our first argument, which left both of us deflated, disappointed, and dejected. I had no idea how to express myself clearly or how to listen to my husband, so the two of us had to put a Band-Aid on our hearts for our wedding day. I began the slippery downward slope to distance between two people who say they love each other.

For years I worked hard to be what I thought was a loving, kind, and fair-minded wife. However, after reading *The Surrendered Wife*, I saw clearly that I wasn't treating my husband with love or respect. My perception of being a great wife was shattered as I came face to face with how I was treating my husband. I nagged him, told him what to do and how to do it, showed a lack of trust in his abilities, and even refused his gifts. As I plowed through the book, I was convinced that Laura not only knew me personally but had followed me around my house, overheard my conversations, perhaps even read my mind. For the first time, I realized that my behavior was creating a marital nightmare for both of us. Although he never spoke of leaving me, I could see that my husband had drifted away and was uneasy and defensive around me. In many ways, our relationship seemed more like a business partnership than a loving, happy marriage. I began to realize that the change I so wanted in our marriage would have to come from me!

One of the first things I learned from the book was how to express my desires. In the past, I had tried wanting what my husband wanted. When I did have a need or desire, I usually didn't express it well or unconsciously used manipulation to try get it. Until this point, I had lacked the awareness that, as Laura teaches in her book, I needed to take responsibility for my own happiness. This was revolutionary to my way of thinking. I realized that I needed to encourage myself to think about my own desires and give myself permission to want things for myself. Once I began to say plainly what it was that I wanted, it opened the door for my husband to become the hero he had always wanted to be for me. By not telling him what I wanted, I hadn't given him the chance to make my dreams come true.

Through the reading and after enrolling in Coach Training, I was learning to say simply and purely what I wanted and then to stop, close my mouth, and, as Laura would say, to "apply duct tape." I even bought a roll of tape decorated with peace symbols and put it on my desk as a reminder to myself. Slowly, I started to see that if I stopped speaking for just a little while, I was giving my husband the opportunity to think for himself and participate in finding a solution. I felt so much peace. I became aware of just how much I usually spoke in our marriage, trying to figure everything out for both of us.

Then, I began to practice having more patience. This was also new for me but had great benefits. It allowed my husband to be more involved without getting told with lightning speed what to do or how to think. If I could refrain from being so quick to control a situation, I would actually gain more participation from him. I can't tell you how many times he's said to me, "Julie, I want you to be happy!" and then taken the initiative to provide what I want. I'm not exhausted by carrying the burden of trying to control everything.

Another revelation I had was that my husband deserved to have his own opinion. We are so different just being male and female. I think I was trying to make him another me much of the time because I thought if he were more like me—drove like me, chose produce like me, bought gifts like me—then we'd get along better. The intimacy principles taught me that this outlook was actually disrespectful. I remember my husband telling me that, for him, respect was like the air he needed to breathe. Yet, I cut off his oxygen at every turn. I had actually adopted a lower opinion of my husband. I was treating him like a child instead of a man. I behaved as if I were the teacher and he were my student. This dynamic did not go over very well, but still I continued out of habit. It wasn't until I learned how to sit back and listen, without judging or interrupting, that he began to open up with me. When I restored his right to be a part of our marriage, I began the process of seeing him as separate from myself and entitled to having a voice and a role in our marriage. I began to elevate him in my mind and heart, and I found him, though different from me, so much more attractive.

My new behavior towards my husband gave me more confidence in him, even though he was the same guy all along! Reading *The Surrendered Wife*, enrolling in the Coach Training Program, and receiving all the benefits from the ongoing support network have helped teach me what respect really looks like. When I gave him the respect he craved, my husband stood a little taller, held his shoulders back, and walked with more confidence. I felt ashamed that I had behaved so disrespectfully out of ignorance and wept when it finally became apparent to me. My husband forgave me when he learned why I was crying, but I also had to forgive myself. Learning how to respect to my husband has given me a sense of dignity about myself that I had never known.

Due to my lack of respect and need for control, problems had also shown up in the bedroom. Rather than revealing my softer side, I was insensitive by complaining about the infrequency with which we made love and his seeming lack of interest in me. Needless to say, the intimacy plummeted. It was no wonder that I felt terribly lonely and rejected, and he seemed uninterested and disconnected. Reading *The Surrendered Wife* encouraged me to relax in the bedroom. I learned how to say what I wanted and be more feminine so that he had an opportunity to love me. By being kind, showing interest, and allowing our time together to be mutually beneficial through expressing my desires, my husband and I have the freedom to enjoy each other with more love and passion than ever.

I am so grateful for Laura Doyle and *The Surrendered Wife*, and so is my husband! In fact, when I enrolled in the Coach Training Program so that I could learn even more and become a coach myself, my husband was all for paying my way! I have to admit that I'm still a work in progress, but I have a supportive group of fellow coaches encouraging me to reach my potential. And now that my husband feels respected and admired, he's eager to support me as I pursue my dreams.

To read more about Julie and test your Intimacy Skills, visit: http://intimacyandpeace.com/julie-koehn/

Chapter 14

Like Teenagers Again

Bonnie Mottram

Certified Relationship Coach, Laura Doyle Connect

Every girl dreams of being swept off her feet by her knight in shining armor. Her vision is that one day she will meet her tall, dark, and handsome man, fall in love with him, marry and bear his children, and live life happily ever after, right? Well, at least that's what I dreamed! My fairy tale romance felt a lot like that dream, at least at the beginning.

I met *my* tall, dark, and handsome man just after graduating from high school. I was already living on my own with roommates. I had a full-time job and a new car that I had just bought on my own credit.

My boyfriend, however, was living at home with his parents. I noticed he managed his money differently than I did. It didn't bother me then, and in his defense, he was just seventeen years old, so he was doing what seventeen year olds do. I figured he had a whole year ahead of him before he had to batten down the hatches and be more responsible. I liked that he had a loving family life, attended church, and enjoyed being around kids.

We dated for nine years before he finally popped the question. Why did it take that long? Did I have anything to do with that extended courtship? I didn't realize it at the time, but looking back I see that I was controlling him on every turn! I was motivated to "help" him learn how to be responsible, like I was, so he would marry me sooner! Little did I know I was only prolonging his decision to marry me because of the way I treated him.

When we finally entered into marriage, we had the wedding that I had always wanted! We decided to have children pretty quickly since we felt ready to take on the role of being parents. Over the next six years, we welcomed two girls and one boy into our family.

I was doing well at work. I loved my profession and often took on management roles. I was given more responsibilities and compensation too. I felt appreciated for the effort I gave at the office and often shared my triumphs with my husband. I participated in my kids' education and extracurricular activities and found leadership roles in those areas too. I also played adult sports and was a co-leader for the sports ministry at our church.

I gladly took charge of our finances. I figured it was the least I could do since he wasn't really a paperwork kind of guy and I already had my own system that seemed to work. My husband was working hard to make ends meet and eventually entered into the family business as a salesman. I felt we would have the financial security that I longed for, so I was happy.

But something was different in my married life. The same skills that worked in my professional life didn't go over as well with my husband. We didn't seem to be on the same page anymore, and our arguments, mostly about our finances or children, were a more frequent occurrence. The only thing I knew to do was tighten the reigns so I could minimize the conflict and any emotional damage that might result from it.

I came up with various plans to curb his spending, which seemed to work for no more than a few months. Soon enough, we were back in the same place: making ends meet but with a lot of frustration and resentment on my part. I was in constant fear about trying to stay ahead of the spending. I expressed to him my fear of not having enough money to pay the bills and told him he was spending irresponsibly. Though I often spent money when and how I wanted to, I would question his purchases when I saw them on the bank statements. I thought I was justified. Somehow I felt it wrong for him to spend but okay if *I* did it.

When it came to parenting, I told him what he was doing wrong and how it should be done. When he played with them on the swing set, I was always right there, telling him not to swing them too high or how to play with them so that they didn't get hurt. I felt I would probably be the one dealing with the hospital or doctor visit, so again I felt justified. Even though I had no history of anything bad happening when he was in charge or playing with the kids, I still questioned his judgment.

When the children were well into their teenage years, he complained that they weren't respecting him and that it was my fault, as though I was telling them how to treat their father. I would just roll my eyes and figured he was blaming me for something that wasn't remotely my fault.

Although we did have fun with our kids and there were other happy times that carried us through, soon our kids didn't want to be home because of the tension they felt between the two of us. My husband started not coming home in time for dinner and made excuses for why he stayed away. When he was home, he was distant and uninterested in conversation, and I really didn't care because I was angry with him anyway. I gave him the silent treatment right back! That tactic didn't seem to be working though because I felt unloved and alone.

At some point, I caught a glimpse of the controlling habits that I had developed over the years. A light bulb turned on for me, and I began to notice that my controlling behavior didn't stop with the finances or the kids. I also saw it when he was driving and I would tell him the best way to go or which exit to turn off, down to the parking stall I wanted him to park in. He would misplace his keys or wallet, so I would gather these items and put them together in the right spot so he would have them when he needed them. He hated me doing this and would often tell me to stop. I only wanted to help! His chief complaint was that I was too controlling. My chief complaint was that if he would just learn from his mistakes, I wouldn't have to control things.

The intimacy was clearly absent in our marriage and had been declining for a while. We sought advice from pastors, family members, married friends, and even marriage counselors. We attended relationship weekends, and I often found myself perusing the self-help section of the bookstore to find the solution to our marital problems. I was out of answers and my working harder to try to make things better only resulted in more despair. I had exhausted every option to save our marriage and after thinking about it, I felt the only alternative we had to a lifetime of unhappiness was divorce. We just couldn't work out the differences between us. So we separated.

I confided in a few close friends, one in particular whom I felt a special connection to. She shared with me the skills of Laura Doyle's Surrendered Wife, Empowered Woman Program. She had given me a book by the same author several years prior, but I read only the first chapter before putting it on my shelf, where it gathered dust for years. She told me about women she knew who had turned their marriages around by using the principles outlined in the program, and she thought it could work for me too. She believed so powerfully in Laura's principles that she nearly guaranteed it and encouraged me to read *The Surrendered Wife*.

I wondered if my friend knew just how controlling I had become, and I worried whether or not my husband would be willing to stay in our marriage long enough for me to give it a shot. Without much hesitation, I agreed. I went home, found the book, wiped off the dust, and began to read. I enrolled in the Coach Training Program and within a week began meeting and sharing with other women who had similar situations. Studying these principles, skill by skill through a powerful weekly training, I began to see a new perspective.

The fact is, I really didn't want a divorce, so I decided to fight for my marriage. I replaced my old habits, one by one, with the new ones outlined in Laura's book and in her training, and I started using the skills immediately in my marriage.

Self-care seemed to be a foreign, unnatural concept to me, but as I began to practice taking time to nurture and care for myself, I noticed something changed. Things I thought were so big and important now seemed small and unimportant just because I was taking care of myself every day using a thought-provoking list I created of things that bring me joy!

I started saying phrases like "whatever you think" when my husband asked for my opinion about something I didn't need to advise him about, or I simply said "thank you" when I noticed him doing something helpful. My heart seemed to soften, and I became less demanding in every area in my life. I felt the change in my husband's demeanor toward me after each new skill I learned. It was almost as if he grew an inch taller with each principle. I realized that this was working—this was really working!

He started coming home on time, cooking dinner again, and greeting me with a smile and a kiss when I came home from work. We seemed to have broken a barrier that had been between us for so long, and I actually felt hopeful that things would continue to fall into place the more I lived these principles.

One particularly great skill taught me how to change my complaints or demands into desires that inspire. Before surrendering, the honey-do list of things undone around the house would drive me crazy, especially when my husband often offered his help to others and their homes rather than fix what was broken in ours. But looking back, when he did do something around the house to try to make me happy or check off the list, I would point out what was wrong with it and where he could have done better, discover part of it that seemed undone, or worse, give him the next thing on the list since he seemed to be on a roll!

I had been complaining about a hole in our ceiling for years. I hardly noticed it anymore, but when I had company over and they pointed it out, I made it seem like it was a current project. With my new skill, instead of complaining about the hole in our ceiling the way I used to, I told my husband that I would really like it if my ceiling was patched so I didn't have to see that hole anymore. It was patched the very next week!

Giving up control after consistently having a tight grip for a long time is not easy. It came as a surprise to see just how much control I had over practically everything. I remember not wanting my husband to go to any trouble to buy me flowers for occasions or holidays because of the expense, and I told him so quite clearly. Then one day, I witnessed a coworker receiving a bouquet of long-stemmed roses, and my heart melted for her. I was so overwhelmed by her joy in that moment that I knew I wanted that feeling myself. But how could I tell my husband that I had made a mistake and now wanted flowers—ideally delivered to my office?

I decided to let him know that I realized I had been silly discouraging him from getting me flowers in the past and that I would learn to embrace his gift of flowers anytime he wanted to be so generous. Since then, I've received flowers many times, sometimes just because! Those are the best kind.

Through these skills, I learned that by passing up a gift from my husband I was missing the chance to connect with him and squashing any chance at making him feel appreciated or thoughtful. I had forgotten what it felt like to receive a gift from someone I adore.

Now, about those finances. I thought about giving my husband the responsibility of managing our money, but I had worked hard to achieve an A+ credit rating and feared that it would decline if he took charge. I read over and over the many benefits Laura described regarding the finances and how my husband would feel accomplished and even proud of providing for his family. Additionally, *The Surrendered Wife* stated that soon after relinquishing control of the finances, I might see a change in his income for the better because he would be aware of the money going in and out of the home. It made perfect sense! I thought, "I should at least try it. Maybe it will work."

Then, as I set the book down and walked away with confidence, my overwhelming fear stepped in and swallowed up those benefits like crumbs from a cookie. I was afraid that paying the bills was my responsibility and that I would be letting him down by refusing to help with my side of our partnership. I felt that I was more efficient, and I knew how he hated paperwork.

Laura suggested that when it comes to relinquishing the finances we not just try it but do it. It was like Laura knew me all too well. In the past I would give something up just to see if my husband could handle it, and then when it didn't go according to my plan, I would take it back as if to say, "I told you so!" I can now see my motives, and they weren't pretty.

I continued to pick the book up to read that section again, week after week, until one day, I just decided it was time to give him the finances. I wanted the benefits more than I wanted to stay in my fear.

I gathered up the bills that were due in the next two weeks. With knees shaking and hands trembling, I laid them on the counter and said, "I can't." "Can't what," he asked. "I can't manage the finances anymore. I just can't do it. It is too stressful." He said, "I understand" and left for work. I thought to myself, now what? I went back to the book and read some more, then called a coach trainee from my program for encouragement.

I walked away from managing the finances that day and have not returned to paying the bills or paying for dinner or even peeking at the checkbook, for that matter!

It wasn't easy, and for a while, I felt like taking it all back and helping him out when he struggled with the new, huge task. But I knew what I would be taking away from him if I did, and that's what kept me from taking over again. I had to trust that my husband is capable of taking care of our family his own way.

Recently, we had an opportunity to get away for a weekend of rest and relaxation. I expressed my desire to go someplace warm and left the details up to my husband. I couldn't have planned it better myself! We wound up in a beautiful beach city a couple hours away where the views were breathtaking and the walks along the sand gave our relationship a whole new meaning. We had lunch in the harbor and he showered me with gifts from my favorite jewelry stores. He remembered the things that made me feel special, and I almost had to pinch myself, thinking it was all just a dream!

The following week, I attended the Cherished for Life Retreat created by Laura Doyle and her staff. They invited a "man panel" as one of the highlights of the weekend. My husband agreed to participate, even though he didn't know what to expect. After a series of questions from the women in the audience, my husband shared about our weekend getaway and how these skills had made all the difference for him in our marriage. With tears in his eyes, he said, "It felt like we were teenagers again!" I truly felt loved, adored, and cherished in that moment, just like my friend had said I would. That's a feeling that I want to hold onto for life!

I realize this is a journey of peaks and valleys in the imperfect world we live in, but if I stay willing and keep progressing, my hope is that I will continue to have the marriage I dreamed of because I have a man who loves me and wants to be his best for me. So far, so good.

I have never looked back, except to see how far I've come since becoming a Surrendered Wife! After almost a year of implementing these skills and going on twenty-nine years of marriage, I can say that it has become my life's mission to end world divorce, helping one woman at a time, and I couldn't be more grateful!

To read more about Bonnie and test your Intimacy Skills, visit: http://intimacyandpeace.com/bonnie-mottram/

Chapter 15

Recognizing My Prince

Sue Prince

Certified Relationship Coach, Laura Doyle Connect

Once upon a time there was a prince named Gregory who came across a fair maiden, Sue. And as the story goes, they were destined to live happily ever after—or so they thought.

Greg and I met on Cupid.com and started corresponding via email. Neither of us was in a hurry to rush into a relationship, so we wrote back and forth for three months before even talking on the phone. By the time we met, we felt we already knew one another. I felt safe and with every date we had, the safety grew. Every word of love in his letters came true as we continued getting to know one another. I felt so cherished and adored, and he treated me like a princess from the beginning. I had never had someone treat me so delightfully. It didn't take long before I knew he was the one I wanted to live the happily-ever-after romance with for the rest of my life.

We were engaged in less than two years, and Greg moved into my townhouse. It was then that the differences between us began to appear. It wasn't really the everyday living things, such as cooking, cleaning, or laundry that caused our struggles. I felt truly blessed and appreciated having found a fifty-five-year-old bachelor who was self-sufficient, independent, and self-motivated. Rather, we struggled with our communication, decision-making, and emotional differences.

I controlled so much in our new life together. Because it was my townhouse, I felt I would continue to make all the decisions regarding the home, along with many other things. I freely gave my controlling opinion about his truck-driving job, which had him on the road for weeks on end. I was a weekend wife and, at least emotionally, not handling it well at all. This only served to make him miserable with regret and unable to make me happy. I was so lonely. And I was becoming exhausted from doing everything while he was gone. Each weekend he would come home, I would have to adjust to his being there. I had my guard up, afraid of being vulnerable to a man who was going to leave me again in a day or two. I was feeling resentful, and he wasn't feeling respected.

We argued whenever we had to make any kind of decisions together. He felt I wasn't hearing him, and I thought he was being self-centered and not listening to me. Whenever we would try to resolve our issues by talking, he would give me his logical approach to everything and say that I was too emotional and was taking things too personally. I would then shut down or explode, and nothing would get resolved. I felt like all of my previous personal growth was fading and my self-esteem was getting damaged. I felt he never heard my opinion, and Greg was feeling the same way about me.

The first year of marriage, we attempted to buy a home together. I had been through the process before and knew what to expect. My husband, on the other hand, had never been through anything like it. It was fast paced and caused a lot of anxiety for Greg. For me, it was the opposite; I was buzzing from all the excitement of finding a home that I loved. Things came to a head when we couldn't agree on negotiations on the house. It caused such a huge fight that we lashed out at one another. There we were, only nine months into our "happily ever after," and he said that he was falling out of love with me! I was crushed. All of my dreams were torn out from under me. I lost it and didn't hold anything back. I began to scream at him and basically told him to get the hell out. He did leave but not before informing me that he was going to stay at a hotel because he felt he was in danger. Ouch! The next day, I called the realtor and our pastor and said goodbye to the home of my dreams.

Once again, I found myself in a failing marriage. It made me ask, "Why is this happening again?" I thought I had found the prince who was going to love me until death did us part. I contacted a marriage counselor recommended by our pastor and made an appointment, desperate to save our marriage. Greg, thankfully, agreed to go. The greatest advice the counselor was able to give to me was a message on a yellow Post-It note: Read *The Surrendered Wife* by Laura Doyle. It was like God working one of his miracles. I had read *The Surrendered Single* a few years before and knew that it was one of the reasons that I found Greg in the first place. So I ran to the bookstore immediately and began to read, desperate for an answer to this insanity that I found myself in.

As I began to read about Laura's marriage, it was like I was reading about myself—especially when she described the control I had over my husband. It got me thinking about my situation, and I discovered that so many of our problems were related to my own fears and insecurities. I knew that I had trust issues, but I didn't realize that I wasn't showing trust in the one person who showed me every day that he adored me.

Even though I totally connected to Laura's book, the hardest thing was to actually start putting the principles into practice. Would they really work for me? Could I get Greg back after I had shown such explosive anger toward him? Could he forgive me? Could I forgive him? I was terrified. I felt desperate to hold onto Greg. My relationship with him was the closest and most compassionate one that I had ever experienced. I truly loved this man. He was a man who could communicate and share his feelings, and he understood the meaning of personal growth. I felt so connected to him, yet we were quickly drifting apart because of all the tension and hostility.

Once I finished reading *The Surrendered Wife,* I decided to take a chance and apply a couple of Laura's simple comments to my conversations with Greg. The first time was while leaving the counselor's office. Greg stated that he didn't think that buying a house was going to make me happy. He had been observing my behavior and saw that when he gave in to try to make me happy, I was restless and wanted more. He was not feeling any gratitude at all from me and wondered how I would ever be happy. While he was saying this out loud, in my mind all I heard him say, very clearly, was "no" to purchasing a home. My defensive walls were up, and I was ready to fight. His words crushed me because I felt another of my dreams quickly receding and hurting our future together in the process. I was thinking at that moment that I should just cash in on this marriage and run away, like I had done so many other times before.

But then I remembered the book, which mentioned respecting my husband. Respecting him did not mean that I must agree with what he says but that I should show consideration for his concerns and his opinions. So I turned to him and stated sincerely, "I hear you." And put the invisible duct tape on my mouth. I'll never forget his response. He let out this huge sigh and said, "Thank you." I was stunned. I realized immediately that he needed to be heard and deeply appreciated the validation of his thoughts. I thought of how that must have felt for him. He may have been thinking, "This woman wants me to make this huge commitment to buy a home with her, yet I never feel heard or respected." His reaction spoke volumes to me that day and helped me see my husband in a totally different light.

The next principle I chose to apply was relinquishing control. Now that I had a better understanding of why I tried to control so much around me, including my husband's actions, I thought this particular skill was needed desperately. I was so overwhelmed with of all the things I felt I needed to control that I was exhausted. Even after he moved in, I continued to do everything I always had but was now trying to run his life too. I didn't give him any opportunity to step in and help with the house, the finances, the pets, or any of the jobs. It was almost as if I were trying to prove to everyone around me that I could be superwoman and didn't need anyone's help.

We had put our house hunting on hold to focus on saving our marriage. After reading the book, I felt that one of the main reasons our marriage was falling apart after less than a year was because of my lack of trust in my husband. I needed to know not only how to settle my fears but how to overcome them as well. I truly didn't realize how little trust I placed in the man I had married or that my past still had a tight grip on my everyday life.

I had tried for years to break free of my past and felt I had done a lot of personal growth, but I never felt there was a true breakthrough until I began knowing myself through God and through His leading me to these principles. I wanted this marriage so badly that I was willing to own up to my part of the responsibility and was even ready to start changing some of my behaviors. In the past when Greg would ask my opinion, I would start giving my ideas and keep going, never allowing him an opportunity to add his two cents. When he did get a moment to say what he thought, I would pooh-pooh his ideas like I knew best, which frustrated him.

When I was presented a situation to try relinquishing my control, I went for it. What did I have to lose? One evening Greg proposed an idea and wanted to know my thoughts around a remodeling project for our townhouse. I paused for a moment and then said, "Whatever you think, honey." He said, "Well, babe, I want you to be able to provide your opinion on this too." And I then said, "I am okay with whatever you think." For the first time in a while, I felt relief pour over me. I was able to hand the decision to Greg and allow him to do the project his way; whatever he wanted to do I was completely okay with. I felt that this was the time to trust Greg with making the decision. He is very meticulous individual and always completes projects that he starts. I knew that I needed to trust that he would likely do a great job. I didn't have to provide my opinion or get into another heated debate on what should be done. I was free from decision-making for the first time in a long time, and it felt great.

I gave him the space to be the man in our relationship and make the decision for us. Before, I felt he was self-centered and that my desires really didn't matter. This experience allowed me to see that his choices are based on both of us and not just what he wants for himself. As I continued to practice this principle, I also began to realize that Greg's suggestions are not necessarily set in stone and that by expressing himself, he was free to think out loud and share his ideas with me. Now I am able to enjoy listening to him and his ideas, to be inspired by his creativity, and to express my desires as well. What a gift this one exercise was for me. I began to see that we actually could have a good conversation without it turning into a frustrating argument.

After a few weeks of practicing the principles, I expressed my desire to begin our house hunting again and added, "What do you think?" Greg said he was sensing a change in our relationship and was willing to reopen that door, which made me ecstatic! We were moving forward again with our future. Stemming from my successful experimentation with the surrendered principles, I knew there was something to hope for in our marriage, and I started searching for more information about Laura. I also knew that it would be a good idea to find like-minded people to support me and keep me accountable, as I wasn't doing the greatest job at remembering to use the principles consistently.

My journey with Laura and becoming a Certified Relationship Coach came from a simple visit to her website, where I provided my contact information. I soon started to receive emails from Laura, but it wasn't until one day, when I got a personal message from her about becoming a coach, that I decided to respond. How many authors would make direct contact with someone who had just read their book? I felt I had to respond and thank her for her offer; however, I had to admit to her that I was not practicing the skills consistently and that I wanted to inquire about meeting others in my area. I didn't feel I was qualified or even a good candidate for her coaching program. We exchanged a few more emails, and she asked if she could call me. *Me?* Talk to an author from California? Wow...

I am so thankful that, following those conversations and inquiries with Laura, I made the decision to become a coach. With her humility and sincerity, I felt an instant trust for and connection with her. I had never met anyone quite like Laura. Her passion to help women feel loved, adored, and cherished by their husbands goes beyond anything I had ever imagined. I chose to follow her mission of ending world divorce and began the Coach Training Program in September 2013. Though my main desire when accepting the invitation to become a coach was to restore my marriage with Greg, I began to see I really could make a difference in other women's lives by leading by example and guiding them in their desire of being loved and cherished by their loved ones.

The training led us through daily practice of the principles and really understanding ourselves, becoming vulnerable with one another and taking that into our home to practice being vulnerable with our husbands. I am able to really feel like a woman by allowing myself to express my hurts rather then put up the defensive walls that I always had before. It's not easy, but being vulnerable is the truth of how I feel. I can show more kindness and gentleness in our relationship as I continue to be vulnerable.

I learned about self-care and that it's okay to treat myself daily to things I enjoy. In fact, it's necessary for a surrendered relationship. In the past, I would ask for permission to do things because I thought that was what was expected of me, even though waiting for a reply would always cause me anxiety. But self-care is about expressing my desires purely. My husband now sees a woman who knows what she wants and goes for it instead of asking if it's okay to do something.

I am learning to respect the man I love. I realized that I actually didn't have a clue what it meant to respect someone. I thought I was very polite and well-mannered. So wasn't that being respectful? I did not understand the concept of respecting someone. I didn't see respect carried out in the house I grew up in. I am so grateful that I have been able to learn what it means to respect and what results come from being respectful.

This journey has been such a huge blessing for both my husband and me. I am changing the way I think and opening my mind to so many glorious encounters with my husband. And, more than ever, I truly see him as the man I love and adore. It feels good to allow him to support me and to trust him to care for me. He has become the prince I always dreamed of having.

And I am so grateful to Laura and all the women I have met and cried with during our time together. I never would have been able to do this without them guiding, supporting, and coaching me through the rough times and the good times. They truly are God's angels!

To read more about Sue and test your Intimacy Skills, visit: http://intimacyandpeace.com/sue-prince/

Chapter 16

Ending The Blame Game

Tatianna Jane Solibun

Certified Relationship Coach, Laura Doyle Connect

"This is a mistake. This can't be happening," I thought to myself as I cried harder in an attempt to make my husband notice that his words had really hurt me. There I was on our bed, with tears streaming onto my already wet pillow. Willie flipped over to the other side, his back towards me. My chest tight and my nose stuffy, I let out heavy sobs. Still he didn't respond. I heaved and cried even harder to make my point clear: I wasn't going to let him sleep in peace until he made things right. He started snoring. By this time, I had gone way past the initial feeling of hurt to anger. I shoved him and said, "See, this is exactly what I mean—you don't even care!" He let out a grunt, turned over drowsily, and started snoring again.

The irony is that, though I had been conditioned to see crying as a sign of weakness, I was determined not to show him how weak I was. I was a married woman now, and I had to get my big girl panties on. I was capable. I could always pick myself up, pack up, and leave him, and I would still be okay, as I often reminded him. My tears usually served as an ultimatum to make him feel guilty, as if they were my trump card. I got even more furious during such episodes and was resolved to keep my tough act—and our marriage—together because I was the more responsible adult around here and surely the smarter one.

I blamed him for being insensitive. I blamed him for not caring enough. I blamed him for not trying harder. I blamed him for not giving me the security I needed. I thought our marriage was a big mistake.

We are two very different people. It's funny how the very things that had drawn me to him when we were dating caused contempt now that we were married. For example, I used to get easily stressed out simply because I was a chronic perfectionist, but his easygoing demeanor helped me relax and trust that things would turn out alright. However, after just a few years into marriage, that very trait began to irritate me, as I started to think he was either lazy or inept. Worse still, when his happy-go-lucky self showed up, I blamed him for being in denial. At the same time, I accused him of being a workaholic, when his hardworking attitude had assured me he would be a good provider in the first place. When we were dating, I loved that he was magnanimous towards others, but now it bothered me that he was over giving.

Throughout episodes of me snapping at him and "helping him change for the better," we would end up in cold wars. Even if he did attempt to make nice, I would push him away to make him try harder. I needed to be convinced that I was worth fighting for. Nothing he did was good enough for me because I believed he could always do better. I thought I was helping him to improve. What I didn't realize was that, instead of making him fight for me, I was making him fight *with* me.

The Fairytale Happy Ending: A Myth?

As a young girl, I witnessed my parents go through a brutal divorce. My fragile heart was shattered even more when my boyfriend cheated and betrayed my trust. In my disappointment, I gave up every hope to be married. But destiny had a different plan. I knew it had to be divine intervention when I met my ex-boyfriend again at church, especially when he wasn't the type to ever step foot into one. I had stricken him off my list of potential suitors. After all, if he had cheated once, wouldn't he do it again? But, not long after starting to serve in a ministry together, we got engaged. We even sought premarital counseling for almost two years, just so I could be sure. And I was. Our wedding turned out to be magical and everything I had imagined it would be. Not long after, however, I took all of that away by wanting to be in control of my marriage. I knew what it was like to grow up in a broken home, and I was determined not to let that happen to me.

In the past, I mistakenly believed that if I rejected the ideas and thoughts I disagreed with, they would disappear and I wouldn't have to deal with any negative consequences. As long as I nipped any "dangerous" ideas in the bud, then I wouldn't have the discomfort of, say, financial insecurity if my husband invested poorly. However, as I have since learned, when we squash someone's ideas, we also kill their spirit.

Years ago, Willie and I were in the car discussing whether he should start a business. He said, "Someday I want to own a music school." I argued with him about how it would be too expensive, too stressful, and too risky because of the economy. Then he responded, "It would be cool to go back to the music industry again," leaving me frustrated because I wanted him to agree that it wasn't a good idea.

What made this already futile conversation truly pointless is that at the time we had just paid off our wedding vendors and could barely pay the mortgage on our new home. We were not having a serious discussion of what to do next. He was just talking, just thinking out loud, and because I didn't want him to think that way I started an argument. If I had known what I know now, I would have simply listened to his vision and responded by saying "I hear you." I didn't have any of the Intimacy Skills then. I didn't know that respecting him meant listening when he talked, really just listening. I always had an opinion or advice to give, but I was demanding and consistently dismissed his ideas.

On the outside, my marriage looked perfect, perhaps even too good to be true, but our intimacy was waning by the day as he started distancing himself from me. Many friends and younger women at church would come up to me and ask in admiration, "How is it that you have it all? A great husband, career, kids. You have everything a woman could ask for." I would manage a smile rather than muttering, "Wait until you get past my front door or take a peek behind the curtains." It wasn't at all about what I had but instead, about the person I had become behind the smile. I was sure if they found out what I was really like, it would repulse them. I wasn't sure if I even liked myself. I knew I wanted a passionate and loving marriage, but I just didn't know how to make it happen. My heart seemed safer locked inside a fortress of steel. I would nudge myself, "Just move on! Get a grip on yourself, for goodness's sake, and get on with being happily married already."

If my marriage was a reflection of who I was, I didn't like what I saw: a controlling, disrespectful, and usually manipulative woman. Deep down, I knew I was acting in response to fear: fear of being disappointed, fear that if things didn't happen my way, I would be taken for granted or be seen as not having my own opinion, fear of not being in control, fear that my husband would leave me for another woman. And I also knew these fears had kept me from being loved and loving freely.

Behind closed doors, I was struggling to keep my act together. Even with more to add to my juggling act, like being a young wife and a new mum, on top of being an aspiring division manager, I didn't slow down one bit to adjust. Instead, I just kept going because my work achievements and perks gave me the quick relief I needed. It was like having a sugar rush when you're hungry. They were enough to keep me going then crash in an emotional heap, only to pick up and run with them again. I could never fully acknowledge the reality of my unhappiness at work or the longing in my heart to connect with my husband. I didn't let those pains scare me enough to reflect on them, let alone deal with them. I had no time for those kinds of thoughts.

While my husband was changing jobs frequently, I had gotten a number of promotions and climbed the corporate ladder rapidly, and was earning a lot more than him. And because I thought I knew better than him, I became arrogant and disrespectful. My tone was condescending as I said the meanest things that would emasculate even the strongest Samson. After our quarrels, although I was left with the terrible aftertaste of having thrown spiteful words at my husband, I would find consolation in rationalizing my behavior (mostly by reasoning "I was just trying to help" or "If only he would do things the way I told him to"). I felt especially bad about myself when I nagged, complained about, or criticized him. But I secretly thought I was superior, that I knew best, and that he had better listen to me.

When we had our first baby, I would tell him what to do. Sometimes he would oblige willingly; other times he would just roll his eyes or brood grumpily. He always seemed to be waiting to be told what to do, to the point that he couldn't even take care of the baby without me, let alone make sure that the diapers were right side out. I saw him as an inept father and began to resent him even more for not taking initiative. What I didn't realize was that I was treating him like a fetch boy who should wait for my orders. No man deserves to be treated that way. I complained to my friends that it was so hard to get him to lift a finger around the house. I didn't feel any better when these rants inadvertently turned into male-bashing sessions. I became exhausted and frustrated.

Our sex life also suffered as a result. He wasn't interested, and even when he did initiate, my resentment was so deep that I ended up feeling used. He wasn't giving me the attention and affection I needed, and I accused him of taking me for granted. I felt he made efforts to get close only when he wanted sex just so *he* could fulfill his physical needs. What about me, my needs? Through my countless rejections, he became more distant and colder by the day. That's when I realized that my husband would rather suppress his needs than be in the same room with a grouchy woman. He couldn't make me happy no matter how hard he tried and nearly stopped trying.

The final straw came when our second son arrived. My already fragile steel armor was caving in piece by piece. I was overburdened in every way possible. Broken, I was left with so many questions that only the small voice in my heart could answer. It had been too long since I'd responded to the whispers of my heart. Now it was screaming in pain that I could no longer ignore. Something had to give.

I remember the morning I handed in my resignation letter. With such a dream job, everyone thought I was insane. I was beginning to think so too, until my thoughts wandered to the altar where I'd made my wedding vows. It had been only five years ago, but I had not felt so alive since. My heart sprang to life as I remembered what it was like again to have a dream come true. I remembered how handsome my groom looked in his suit as he waited for me at the end of the altar with his best men. I saw an ambitious, capable, caring, and smart man standing there. A man I could see myself spending the rest of my life with. A man I could see fathering my future children. A man who loved my family in spite of our loudness and imperfections. My heart danced as I pledged my love to him for better or for worse, until my dying breath.

Sadness overwhelmed me as I thought about the stark contrast between that feeling and the present. Exhaustedly going through the motions with a dark cloud over his head, Willie was now but a shadow of that groom. My eyes stung as hot tears rolled down my cheeks onto the bible in my hand. I sat at my desk staring at the blurred and soggy pages, disillusioned and confused about how it had all turned out like this. Our marriage was dying. Instead of lovers, we were adversaries trying to prove a point to each other. My numb heart was now desperate to break free. There had to be a better way, and I was determined to find it. Praying in my heart, "God, help me," I got up from my desk with the bible in one hand

and instinctively picked out *The Surrendered Wife* with the other from the bookshelf where it sat neatly tucked away. As I began flipping through the yellowed pages, it confirmed what I already knew, and I wrote to Laura. I was finished running away from broken hearts, and I began to understand how a heart that breaks open can contain the universe. It was during this darkest time of my life that I learned about who I am and that led me to the satisfying relationships I enjoy today.

Just as Laura claims, learning the Intimacy Skills is one of the most rewarding self-improvement projects that I've undertaken. I came to realize I wasn't alone. Like many women around the world, I recognized that as long I had the illusion of control, intimacy had little chance to thrive in my marriage or other relationships. But when I learned to stop controlling others, practice gratitude, and focus on self-care, the atmosphere at my home changed. I became empowered to take responsibility over how I was feeling rather than blaming those around me. This took the pressure off my husband to make me happy, and as a result, brought the fun and laughter back into our marriage. Our playfulness helped me not to sweat the small stuff like I had before. With a good dose of self-care, I started feeling at ease and lighthearted around him, to the point that it was hard not to see each other in a kinder way.

While away on holiday recently, I had forgotten to cancel our housecleaning services. The agency called to say that they had waited outside for two hours and that we would be charged anyway. I felt foolish to have forgotten something like that, and when I told my husband about it, he tenderly said, "It's okay, dear; we all make mistakes. We'll just pay them when we get back." In the past, the guilt that came with minor slip-ups like these would trigger me to start a finger-pointing battle. Worse still, if he had been in my shoes, he would have gotten a no-mercy lecture. I didn't have the grace to allow for mistakes and be as accepting as I am now.

As I revisit painful moments of the past, I can't pinpoint what our fights were even about. I had let myself get so emotionally depleted trying to be the noble martyr that he always seemed an easy target for my misery. It wasn't fair to let him have all the fun, especially when I wasn't giving myself permission to have any. I gave him a hard time every time he wanted to hang out with the guys or make time for his weekly futsal game. He was practicing good self-care, but I felt he was ditching me for his friends. Early in my surrendering journey, I noticed how he would sheepishly ask me for "permission" to go out. Until then, it had never occurred to me how much of a mother-son dynamic I had created in our marriage. No wonder he always waited for me to tell him what to do.

One time I put off self-care for a few days to stay home with my two boys. I felt guilty for not being there as their mother. I didn't want to be "selfish" and decided to sacrifice my own care. But lo and behold, when Willie got back from work, he was greeted by a grumpy, resentful and a walking time bomb of a wife. Stretched beyond my limits, I wasn't much good to anyone, including myself. I was snappy at the slightest scribble outside the lines, so much so that I could almost hear my sons breathe a sigh of relief as they looked up from their art books to the hero who had just walked in. The minute my husband opened the front door, they ran for their lives towards him, screaming with glee! I can now laugh about it, but that day I ended up sacrificing a peaceful and intimate relationship with my family.

At the time, the idea of having some me time sounded absurd, especially for a mother with a toddler and an infant in tow. The notion of self-care seemed counterintuitive because it was like asking me to give what I didn't have and wanted most: more time and more of me to go around. I couldn't see how to make time for the mani-pedi that I was dying to have, especially since I had Mount Washmore to conquer in the laundry room and never-ending messes to clean on the floor. However, in spite of the guilt of feeling irresponsible for taking time out for myself, I decided to give it a one-week trial. I soon realized the value of having my emotional tank filled in order to nurture intimacy with my family. I am more patient and kinder when I know my giving is out of the overflow of my tank rather than depleted reserves.

I remember taking up Zumba classes as part of my self-care. It was a rare occurrence at the time, but I left Willie alone to handle the kids without any detailed instructions. When I got home, the kids had already eaten lunch and were happily watching TV. Of course, it wasn't the way I would have done it, especially when I learned they'd had instant noodles and chips for lunch. I had to make a conscious choice about how to respond: I could lecture Willie about how instant noodles had no nutrition for growing children and show him (as if he didn't already know) where the educational, brain-engaging toys were or I could be grateful that I'd had the morning off, felt feminine dancing, and had a nice lunch with my girlfriend. I'm glad I kept the peace by choosing the latter. After all, no one broke a bone or lost a tooth that day. Everyone was happily alive and in one piece.

It has been three years since I started incorporating the skills and principles in my life and, like any new skill, they weren't easy at first. But with the right support network, they are completely attainable for every woman. My husband and I enjoy so much more peace as a couple now that we see eye to eye with respect and love. I know that I don't have to agree entirely with his way of doing things, but I honor his choices, big and small, and meet his efforts with respect. Rather than dwelling on what's wrong, I've learned to focus on gratitude and replenishing myself.

I used to think that working for the family was the most basic responsibility a wife should expect of a husband. However, since my dysfunctional spouse-fulfilling prophecy was "He can never get anything right," I accused him of spending too much time at work and not enough time at home. The skills taught me how gratitude can really change our world through the lens we look at it with. I still remember the look on my husband's face while I held onto his arm as he was leaving for work one morning. As he turned to look at me, I said, "I wanted to thank you... Thank you for working so hard to provide for the kids and me." He had this look of simultaneous shock and relief that said, "She *finally* gets it!" I realized I'd been swollen with a sense of entitlement, something I wasn't proud of. And really, who wants to be intimate with a woman who treats you like a workhorse? The amazing thing is that ever since, he makes it a point to come home early enough to have dinner as a family and get the kids to bed. He also surprised me by initiating regular date nights where he handles most of the planning, from deciding where we're going to making babysitting arrangements.

My husband is a great father, parenting our two boys the way only a daddy can. It turns out that things don't always have to be mummy's way. He initiates home improvements and takes tremendous pride in helping me around the house. He is my best support and most trustworthy confidant. I learned to trust him again with respect, listening to his ideas (no matter how loony they may sound sometimes) rather than shooting them down. I've begun to see how his ideas can actually be better than mine and give me perspectives that I may otherwise have overlooked. It's magical to know that when I surrendered, the connection I once craved was within reach. My marriage is really like a dream come true again.

I learned what it means to be my best self. The more feminine I am, the more it brings out the masculine side of my husband. I also learned to build more fulfilling relationships with other women, which seemed so simple with the skills. The best part is seeing how the skills have positively affected my children too! The culture around our home these days is one of gratitude for each other and the safety and humility that come with being able to admit when we don't always get it right. My journey of surrender is like a homecoming. I was once reluctant to thank my husband even for little things for fear that he would stop doing them altogether or that I would sound subservient. Instead, thanksgiving is what fills the cup of our family life. It is rewarding to see this skill trickle down even to our two boys, who constantly thank us. Gratitude brings to life what abundance means for us, where before the focus was on complaints and what we didn't have. It does not mean having everything in the world but is made up of moments throughout the day when we choose to appreciate and be present together.

Where I once thought being vulnerable was weak, I now consider it one of my strengths. I learned to live from my heart again, and my mind knows when it's safe to let my guard down, especially in relationships where fostering intimacy is a priority. Sure, I am tempted to react in anger at times, but normally I allow myself to reach for the hurt inside. Crying in front of my husband is now healing for me, as it doesn't come with accusations or blame. My tears are met with his comfort and tenderness. Responding with an "ouch!" when he has said something hurtful is also helpful (and certainly feels more dignified than throwing a bag of cereal at him, as I once did).

I surrendered the feeling of being in control and now experience the liberty of being empowered. I feel whole, my mind finally connected to my heart. Most importantly, I am free to embrace being feminine in my family, marriage, business, and parenting.

To read more about Tatianna and test your Intimacy Skills, visit: http://intimacyandpeace.com/tatianna/

Chapter 17

Where Harmony and Intimacy Reign

Leticia Vasquez
Certified Relationship Coach, Laura Doyle Connect

When I was seventeen, I had had my heart broken in the worst way. When that happened, I donned an armor of protection and decided that no one was going to break my heart again. Like many women, I went on to make a list of the qualities I wanted in my perfect mate. I rejected every single good guy who approached me. They were really nice men but were always missing something: not tall enough, smart enough, funny enough. After nine very lonely years, on the eve of my twenty-sixth birthday, I decided that I did not want to live alone for the rest of my life. For the first time in my adult life, I admitted to myself that I wanted to be in love. And I took off that armor. Very soon, I met my amazing husband. And we lived happily ever after!

Well, there were a few detours in that happily ever after. I met my husband in 1997, and we got married in 1999. It was love at first sight all right—my sight. I'll never forget that first tender moment I opened the door to him when he came to visit my roommate. He marched right past me and headed straight for a second roommate, who was in the post-asthma attack episode she was prone to having. This gentle man disarmed me with his concern. While we told him that the asthma sufferer herself insisted that she be left alone after an episode, he persisted in grabbing blankets and pillows to comfort her. My five roommates and I looked guiltily at each other. And that was it for me—I knew I had found my guy.

We had a beautiful romance, and in my eyes, we were the perfect couple. I had grown up with a healthy sense of self, thanks to my very loving family. I had a wonderful father. And since women often model their romantic partners on their fathers, my future husband was an amazing man. I had to work a little bit to convince him that I was his dream girl though. We were students, him in his early twenties and me a whopping four years older. And we lived on separate continents, before the advent of Skype, text messages, and cheap phone calls. Our romance was filled with biweekly letters and Sunday phone calls, full of breathless and teary *I love you*'s.

By anyone's account, I have always been daddy's little girl. I was the youngest of three children and the family bonus, as I like to call it. My father loved me and continues to love me with a love so deep that we needn't say much to each other to know what we're thinking. There was no childhood whim that he would not try to satisfy. He hated to see me sad yet would quietly chuckle at my moodiness. My nickname? "Raging Bull." No, not something to be proud of, but my parents thought it was cute. Upon meeting my parents, my husband told them that he realized I was a little gruff around the edges but that he was confident he could melt that away in time. My dad laughed, while my husband was left scratching his head. It wasn't until a few years later that he understood what my father meant. Undeterred at first, my husband put up with my domineering behavior for five mostly blissful years.

During those early years of our relationship, I made all the decisions: what we ate, who we befriended, what we did on weekends. And if I wasn't in charge, I pouted, I moped, I grumbled. Even worse than deciding whom we socialized with and how we spent our money was how I talked to him. I informed him of things. For example, I remember telling him, "By the way, on Friday night, I'm going out to dinner with Lynn. I'm not telling you in order to ask for permission; I'm only telling you so that you're not surprised." This in the presence of his own friend, who paused and said, "Wow. What a statement." And what did my husband say? All he said was "Okay."

My lovely husband trudged full speed ahead, speaking quickly to somehow convince me that his idea was a good one. I had a retort for all of his comments, a counter-suggestion for anything he stated. And worst of all, rules for everything, such as these golden oldies: "Leave no dishes on the counter, and dry and put all dishes away. Make the bed every morning. It gives order to a house and to a day."

This type of communication escalated to the point where he got tired of being a doormat. By that time, I had completely emasculated him, and when he started defending himself, I knew we were in trouble.

After six years of my controlling everything in our relationship, my husband said enough was enough. He couldn't take my dominating behavior anymore. He decided that if I didn't change, the relationship was over. His making this decision was a shock. How could the beloved I had worked so hard to find and cultivate have changed his mind? My initial reaction was that it was over, that getting back together would be an act of submission tantamount to letting down all women the world over. If he felt so strongly, maybe it was best to let him go. There were other fish in the sea.

Only I didn't want other fish.

As it turned out, after a three-month separation, neither did he. We decided to stay together because we agreed that we were the best things that had happened to one another, and we wanted to share our lives together. So a new relationship was born. Only this time, my emasculated husband wanted to make decisions. Even though I agreed, the walk was much harder than the talk, and I still insisted on making most of the decisions. What followed was a decade of incredible highs and incredible lows.

On one occasion, after studying fourteen hours a day for three months, I sojourned to Albany, New York, to take the bar exam. Upon my return to our Washington, DC, apartment, my husband had a rental car waiting and the bags packed. I was so upset because all I wanted was to unwind at home. I hated surprises, and I fumed the entire three hours to a beautiful cabin he had booked for us in West Virginia. I look back to that moment and am so ashamed of myself!

We changed continents and headed for the Netherlands, a new country, new language, and new culture for both of us. We united in the face of so much unfamiliarity. After a few years, it wasn't so new anymore, but then we had our first child. Along with more teeth clenching amidst the beauty of a new baby came a new round of commitments as we bore witness to the miracle (and responsibility) of bringing another human being into the world. And a new set of rules by a mom who knew exactly nothing about raising a child but still wanted to be in charge. On we waltzed and tripped.

For the next five years, we alternated between romantic and stone-cold weekends owing to my absolute need to control everything. Finally, one night my husband arranged for a babysitter so we could go to a romantic restaurant. He apologized for his behavior, and I apologized for mine. We agreed that we needed to change our relationship drastically because we knew there was no one else we wanted to share our lives with. This commitment was different; there was a sense of graveness about it, steeped in firm resolve. We knew our futures depended on it, and we took it seriously. He had his list of what hurt him most about my behavior; I had mine. We resolved to do all we could to address these issues.

I came across lots of books and philosophies on the perfect

marriage at bookstores and online. Some were too generic: Practice mindfulness. Love everyone. See the beauty in all things. Do yoga. Use the classic work-related model for conflict resolution ("When you do x, I feel y"). Some were too academic: the amygdala hijack and our lack of reaction to anything or anyone when the hijacking takes place. The information was fantastic, but it was all too broad for me. I loved what I read, but in the heat of the moment, while I could see my amygdala throbbing and the Dalai Lama's peaceful face, I simply couldn't resist "expressing myself." I thought I was doing just that—expressing myself—and it did feel good to let go, but the silence and sadness left in its wake were numbing. After the initial feelings of smugness subsided, an emotional hangover descended upon me.

And then I found Laura Doyle on Amazon.com. She beckoned to me, but I couldn't do it. Until I realized that all those other books were not having much of an impact on my communication style. Finally, I relented and thought, "What the heck? I have nothing left to lose." I read the first few pages online, took her quiz, and shrieked at how controlling it said I was. And after months of pondering, I bought the *Surrendered Wife*. But shhhhh, it was a secret.

The confusion over being a "Surrendered Wife" is astounding. Look at Laura's reviews, and you'll see them there, among the many positive ones. Laura's basic premise is to let go of wanting to control what you cannot control. Namely, you can control your own behavior but no one else's. That's simple enough. And it's easier said than done. At the beginning of this process, when my husband made his typical major offenses (like dressing the kids in stained clothes, not stacking the dishes a certain way, or not taking the direct route to the airport), I said nary a word. It was not easy, but I was determined. After about two weeks of keeping the duct tape on my mouth, not saying anything when he committed these offenses, my husband asked me what was going on and said that he loved seeing the easygoing gal he had met twenty years earlier. That was it for me. That's when I knew I was well on my way to learning the immense pleasure and power of letting go of my need to control most everything.

Before surrendering, nothing could make me angrier than coming home to find that any of the tasks on my to-do list that had not been done (my way). Any of these violations could immediately trigger what I used to call my "Godzilla mode": I would storm around, huffing and puffing, angrily asking the still air around me why I was the only responsible person in the house, slamming doors as I conducted a thorough inspection of our house. And then, as quickly as Godzilla had arrived, she would leave, with utter destruction in her wake. For the first five minutes after any of these scenes, I would congratulate myself for being in the right and for expressing myself. Then, about twenty minutes later, those feelings of righteousness would transform into regret. And one hour later, there I was, begging my husband to talk to me, trying to convince him about why I was right (and he was wrong). But it was too late; my husband was gone, and his cold silence could last for days. Our record was five days. The worst part was that I did this, on average, every eight days. I know because I counted.

Since surrendering, Godzilla has yet to return, and with her those cold silences have also departed. I still get angry sometimes, but I always ask myself if it's worth exploding and losing the intimacy in our relationship. I can tell you that it never is! And you know what? My kitchen is usually clean when I come home from being out (though it's usually my husband's version of clean, not mine). And on the occasion that it's no one's version of clean? I simply let it go. Screaming is not worth the loss of intimacy I'm so happy to share with my husband and children now. My transformation began with trusting my husband and not wanting to control everything.

My controlling behavior was not the only issue in my marriage. Before surrendering, I couldn't receive graciously. So when my husband came home with a gift, I had a routine: smirk then make a negative statement. I don't think I ever received a gift graciously from my husband before surrendering. There was always something wrong with the gift:

- Flowers? They die so quickly.

- Shoes? I haven't worn heels in years. I can't walk in them anymore.

- Panama hat? Not warm enough to wear in this cold city. Better a beanie.

- Chocolate? Thanks, but you know I eat only dark chocolate.

- A meal out? Oh, how much we could have saved had we cooked this at home.

- Lingerie? Too tight.

And then the air would go still. And my husband would go away in sadness. That was my gift-receiving routine.

Looking back, it pains me to think of the hurt I caused him. It hurts me even more when I try to dissect my own motivation for behaving like a spoiled child. Daddy's little girl syndrome? Not getting what I really wanted? Not wanting to be the center of attention? The frequency of the gifts diminished over time. How could it not? In the end, my reasons didn't matter. I was hurting the person I loved most who, despite my flat-out rudeness, kept on wanting to shower me with attention.

Fast forward to surrendered me: I beam while my husband hands me a gift. Sometimes, he surprises me. Sometimes, he lets me know in advance because he can't wait to hear my excitement, even if over the telephone. And when I look at the gift, whether a five-euro flowerpot or a fifty-euro voucher, I am genuinely happy—and grateful.

- Flowers? They are so beautiful and make our home so bright.

- Shoes? I now have so many to choose from. Lucky me!

- Panama hat? That green one gets rave reviews!

- Chocolate? A smaller piece of milk chocolate is better for me!

- A meal out? Yay, no cooking or cleaning!

- Lingerie? Turn the lights out!

Finally, surrendering helped me to face something I had long struggled with: our sexual intimacy. After years of telling myself that I would do something about my low libido, surrendering finally made me seek professional help. While my doctor and the sexologist fumbled with my paperwork when I arrived for my appointment (much to my mortification), I realized that discussing it aloud actually made something in my own brain click. I had let my femininity go in the name of aging, being a busy mom, and not wanting to be seen as frivolous.

I asked myself some questions and experimented: What defines femininity for you, Leticia? Sparkly lip gloss? High heels? A beautiful silk dress? Manicures? Chanel No. 5? I had abandoned my femininity years ago, thinking those things so trivial in a world with serious problems. With a steely resolve, I rediscovered it. Once I began surrendering, I remembered, at the age of forty, how to wear heels again. I felt absolutely ridiculous as I counted the years I likely had left to wear heels and wondered if it was worth it. Well, the shine in my husband's eyes was worth it—and even led to getting my ears pierced at forty-three. Now it's all I can do to stop him from coming home with presents for me. He loves seeing me so feminine. And you know what? I love it too.

Of course, surrendering is not about being sexy, getting gifts, and saying yes to everything my husband wants. No, it's much more empowering than that. And the Intimacy Skills all work together: when one puzzle piece falls into place, the others start falling into place as well. Surrendering has made me nothing like the Stepford Wife I thought was on the jacket of that book I surreptitiously bought. And nothing can make me prouder than being able to identify a surrendered moment today and compare it with before.

On a recent Saturday morning, my husband told me his sister was coming over for brunch. My two boys had Saturday morning football practice, so off we went, and I consciously left my keys at home, knowing he'd be home whenever we returned from practice.

I called him from the football field to let him know, and he assured me that he'd be home. When the boys and I returned, my husband was not in fact home and, naturally, I was locked out. With two tired young ones.

I called my husband, and he said that he and his sister had changed their minds and gone into town. I told him I'd catch up with him by car to pick up the keys. I called twice to let him know exactly where I was at that moment, as he was on a busy one-lane street. During the third call, when I was finally on his street, he shouted at me on the phone that I knew he didn't like this kind of disorganization, that he hated when I did things like that, etc. I was so hurt. He had hung up on me, so there as no time to say "ouch." I thought I was being helpful by telling him how close I was getting, but he found it incredibly annoying (yes, controlling disguised as helping him out). I saw him and his sister on a busy street corner, and we exchanged keys. No time for a chat. I cheerily thanked him and left. And fumed.

For the next two hours, I thought about several clever responses: text him a long message, leave an even longer one on his voicemail, go out with the kids for the rest of the afternoon. Luckily, I stopped myself and decided to have a bubble bath. I walked into my bedroom and there, on top of my neatly made bed, was a beautifully wrapped gift that he had brought back from Barcelona the night before. I was overcome with a wave of gratefulness. My anger subsided. I texted him a very different message than the one I had imagined two hours before. This one was full of thanks. He immediately responded by saying that he hoped I'd be home in an hour because he had found something beautiful for me, in just my size. Two hours later, he came home bearing a beautiful dress. We had a date with friends, so I quickly donned it and went on to receive so many compliments. We came home laughing and hugging, all affection for one another. I went on to have a sleep-filled night and awoke ready for a wonderful and relaxed Sunday, which started by him bringing me breakfast in bed.

Now I understand that as women, we are often bombarded with

messages of our superiority over men. An abundance of advertisements and magazine articles portray women smirking over their partners' inability to take care of their children, to stop and ask for directions, to remember where the Band-Aids are. The thinking goes that since we are so in touch with our feelings and those of others *and* capable of bringing life into the world, we are nothing short of superwomen. Don't get me wrong—I love the feminine traits that we women possess. I love how we can open up to each other, how we organize nights out, family events, and shopping days, and how our eyes get glossy as we watch our children play soccer. How we laugh together, how we cry together. And our silences that are full of emotion. I love it all. However, the pressure to adhere to the Superwoman image, in my opinion, is not serving us well. I would like to declare I am not Superwoman! I am not perfect; I do not have all the answers.

The reality is that, as a woman, I have attained some pretty amazing things. I was lucky enough to have been born into a loving family, the last of three children. I have siblings who I love and who demonstrate their love for me to no end. I have aunts, uncles, cousins, and friends who enrich my life in more ways than I can count. I have healthy relationships with the people I value most. But no one is more important to me than my husband, not even my children. As shocking as that may sound, I know that the greatest gift I can give my two sons is a happy and healthy relationship with their father.

Now that surrendering is a permanent part of my life, harmony and intimacy reign in our lives. We're back to being that awesome couple we were when we met, with the laughing, the chatting, the hugging (and yes, the sex). All of it. Just wonderful.

To read more about Leticia and test your Intimacy Skills, visit: http://intimacyandpeace.com/leticia-vasquez/

Chapter 18

From Surrendered Single to Surrendered Wife

Katherine Wong-Velasco

Certified Relationship Coach, Laura Doyle Connect

I was fortunate to start my surrendering journey before marriage. Learning to surrender is one of the biggest gifts I ever gave to myself. My surrendering journey has been exciting and rewarding.

Before I started coaching women on their relationships, I was a Human Resources Manager and an Executive Recruiter who paired talented professionals with multinational corporations. I saw myself as a kind and helpful person who was easy to work with. My colleagues described me as hardworking, organized, and highly efficient. I had explored exotic hobbies and traveled to and lived in many different cities throughout the world. I felt comfortable initiating conversations with strangers, and the relationships with my family and friends played a major part in my life.

Since I was young, I liked to plan things and keep everything under control. The idea of surrendering in any sense was a scary concept. Throughout my young adult years, I pushed myself both professionally and personally by setting goals to achieve specific milestones by a certain age. For example, I told myself to complete my MBA by the time I was thirty-five, and I received the degree when I was twenty-nine. I aspired to a career level with a six-figure income before I was forty and achieved it at 34. I was creating a life for myself that some people only dream of, and I felt very good about who I was and how much I had accomplished.

I also planned to be married and have children by the age of thirty. Though I was ready to settle down, when I celebrated my thirtieth birthday I was still unmarried. My friends thought I would be the first one to get married after college because I was surrounded by men in my social and professional environments. I thought so too. But I had no clue why love was not happening the way I had planned. I applied my ambitious work mindset to dating. But when I did date, the men seemed either to be interested only in sex or to be as controlling as I was. Often, I'd hit it off with a man initially, only to have it fizzle just as fast. It became increasingly clear that the chance of meeting the perfect man was slim because I was so picky.

I didn't realize that I had been controlling things by choosing to go out with only certain types of men. For example, any man I dated must work at a reputable organization, drive a certain kind of car, or have gone to a prestigious university. I once dated a guy who went to the same college as I did, and I thought his social status and financial stability matched my expectations. Yet, he was not kind to others or me and, it turned out, he was a chronic cheater. Dating became almost daunting. Often, my dates were not much fun because I was too busy pretending to be someone I was not, trying to convince him (or myself or maybe both of us) that I was easygoing and open to finding lasting love.

When I did start seeing someone seriously, it didn't take long for me to start controlling his life too. I would clean his home or stock his refrigerator with healthy food. But this controlling behavior got me no closer to finding the lasting love that I was seeking. I was only being regarded as someone who was overdoing and over-giving. When I got tired of it and felt taken advantage of, the resentment would overwhelm me. As a result, I brought negative energy into my relationships and then they would fall apart.

Like many women, I opened myself to the advice from gossip magazines and girlfriends. However, the suggestions I heard and read about weren't practical and led me nowhere. One girlfriend told me to use sex to keep guys interested, which was not helpful at all.

I first heard about surrendering through Laura Doyle's books. That day, I announced that another relationship had failed. I went to a local bookstore and explored the self-help section. Right away, *The Surrendered Single* got my attention. Since I valued efficiency, I went straight to the chapters that seemed the most practical for my situation. One chapter in particular, "Make Yourself Happy Every Day," sounded like the perfect recipe for me. I could not recall when the last time I had done something nice for myself was. But just as quickly, my old thinking kicked in and I wondered, "Isn't that a bit selfish?" I felt much more comfortable being the giver in the relationship.

But I decided to give it a try anyway. In the beginning, as I was coming up with my list of twenty things that I could do to make myself happy, as suggested in the book, I had difficulties coming up with ideas. But the book said anything that made me happy when I was doing it or after I had done it should be considered self-care. How about redoing my nails? Or taking a nap after lunch? I started doing three self-care actions a day and had so much more energy. I felt far more tolerant of the frustrations from dating and was even becoming more patient at work. From then on, I had no doubt that self-care was essential to making my life happier, and I kept doing three self-care acts each day.

Another chapter that got my attention was titled, "Accept Dates with Men You Normally Wouldn't Go Out With." This was a tough one! I could see it was compelling advice for me, but I found it hard to put into practice because of my expectations that a man have a similar background as mine. I decided to examine my insistence that any man I dated fit a certain mold. Upon reflection, this idea was governed by my own fears. For example, when I feared not having enough money to survive, I was desperately driven to be successful at school and work so that I could guarantee my own income. I wanted the men I dated to be equally or more successful than I was. There I was, being controlling again. I was beginning to see that when I tried to control the types of men I would date, as well as the outcome, that was when I felt the most frustrated in my search for romance.

It took me several weeks to accept dates that I never would have in the past. I got some funny stories out of it, but it wasn't that bad! I survived. Once, I went out with a guy who I was introduced to by a matchmaker. Although he seemed to enjoy lunch with me, he did not ask for my contact information afterward. He was honest when he told the matchmaker that he wasn't interested in me. That was fine with me. My heart wasn't broken, and I found that I enjoyed the time that I had with these potential boyfriends.

On a first date with another gentleman, I mentioned that I liked using olive oil on my salad. On our second date, at a nice Italian restaurant, he brought me a souvenir from his business trip: a one-liter bottle of olive oil from Turkey! I was surprised at his attention to detail in recalling this simple statement. It was fun to date different types of men, learn their stories, and allow them to pamper me. It was also nice to listen my heart more. Instead of keeping track of what criteria they met or didn't meet, I was able to simply enjoy the time spent with them, and I no longer made suggestions about how they could organize their kitchens!

I realized that the relationship of my dreams would never happen if I tried to force it, so I learned how to enjoy being taken care of without controlling what would happen next. I focused on enjoyment and intimacy instead of calculating how well they fit my previous expectations. I also stopped comparing my success with theirs, which had been driven by my notion that being an independent woman would attract more men. I started listening to what the men had to say and noticed the small things. It was so nice to let go, relax, and allow my potential suitors to find out more about me by asking questions instead of trying to give them all of the information I thought they wanted to hear.

I also started to respect men in general by appreciating them more. It occurred to me that there were things I felt only they could do—like gadget maintenance, killing cockroaches, and other manly things—and I didn't need to outsmart them. I also learned to keep my mouth shut and just listen to my heart. Did I enjoy spending time with him? I used to list the discrepancies between a perfect guy and a so-so guy so that I could protect myself from heartbreak. But there's really no way to do such an investigation in the first few dates and the men's personalities were all so unique, so I started to accept these men for who they were. Once I began to understand that control was a symptom of my fears—of being rejected, getting hurt, or losing intimacy—I gradually learned to let go. If I truly wanted to find my perfect guy, I was going to have to risk my heart a bit.

My past relationships weren't mistakes; they were learning experiences to grow from. After speed dating, matchmaking, and taking suggestions from friends and family, I attracted the most wonderful man, who later became my husband. We were introduced through common friends. I thoroughly enjoyed every date with him. He was good at making me laugh and protecting me. He pampered me with gifts. He cared about my well-being. Though we were very different people, this difference is something I appreciate deeply. There is a way to be happy inside that difference because men and women are just meant to be different.

He was one of the guys who I enjoyed dating without any marriage agenda. About a year after we met, I knew clearly what I wanted: a family. But it was not because of my fear of being lonely or a desire for financial stability. I simply loved being with him and enjoyed our relationship. We finished breakfast the morning of my birthday, and I told him about my wish of spending my life with the man I love. His response caught me off guard. I thought he would have one of the only two responses: "*Yes*, I want to spend my life with you" or "*No*, I don't want to spend my life with you." Instead, he said, "Aren't we spending our lives together now?" He was right. We were spending our lives together, but I also wanted to be married and have children, a critical desire that I had not expressed. Since I had missed the opportunity to say that, in addition to spending my life with the man I love, I also wanted to have kids one day, he questioned why I wanted to get married.

Actually, I was not entirely sure why I wanted to get married. So when we didn't reach a conclusion about where the relationship should go, I thought we should take a break from seeing each other. Since we lived in different cities at the time, the next time we could see each other was a month later. It was then that I suggested we pause our communication. It wasn't an ultimatum that he needed to marry me immediately but just a break to cool down from the heated conversation about marriage. In that cooling-off period, I focused my energy on myself again by practicing great self-care. I reflected on my desire to get married, and I was sure that I did not fear loneliness anymore. I felt serene and trusted that the universe would bring me what I desired. I also knew that even if it turned out we were not to be, I'd survive and attract the next man. In any case, I was grateful for the wonderful time spent with him.

A month later, he proposed! What an amazing reward for letting go and trusting that things would be okay, while also staying feminine and surrendered!

I still practice the Intimacy Skills daily. The phrase "whatever you think" is difficult to say, but when I keep my mouth shut after he asks for advice, he likes it. I also apologize when I accidentally do give him advice. Each time I apologize, he just holds me and says, "It's okay."

Being vulnerable isn't easy either. I had never cried in front of my husband, but when my dad was hospitalized, I let the tears pour out. My husband did not think crying meant that I was weak but saw it as an opportunity to hold me, comfort me, and be there for me.

I frequently express my desires, which my husband sees as more opportunities to show that he is listening and cares about me. Not long ago, I said that I loved when he gave me gifts and asked me out, like when we were dating. Today, he still asks me out on dates and brings me gifts. Who says men are less romantic after becoming husbands? As someone who did not know how to accept people's generosity, now I feel so comfortable accepting this from my husband.

When our first child was on the way, he took excellent care of me. He made sure that I was home safe every day and helped around the house. After the baby was born, sometimes I would turn into a controlling mom who was very protective of the baby. If I wanted things done a certain way, like the breast milk to be reheated at certain temperature, I told him what to do. I would apologize immediately because it was controlling and disrespectful. If I hadn't learned the surrendering skills, such conversations could easily have turned into big fights.

Our love lives need support. There's so much confusion in the dating world and plenty of clashes to work through when it comes to engagement and marriage. Haven't we all felt misunderstood at some point or found it hard to understand even ourselves? Seeking support was my first step to a healthy, intimate relationship. No man or woman is an island, and problems with intimacy and emotional connection cannot be solved alone. Where a hurdle may seem impossible, Laura and her team of Certified Relationship Coaches can show that it's just an obstacle to overcome. All you need is the willingness to make a change, and you, too, can have the thriving, intimate relationship you've always wanted.

To read more about Katherine and test your Intimacy Skills, visit:
http://intimacyandpeace.com/katherine-wong-velasco

Acknowledgements

I'm so grateful for my amazing husband John Doyle, who saw my vision for this project from the beginning and has been nothing but supportive.

I also want to especially thank my patient and talented copywriter, Megan Askew, for providing structure, support, and encouragement. Megan's clarity and attention to detail carried our coaches and me along when we needed it most. Without Megan, this book would not be possible. I'm incredibly grateful for her tireless shepherding of this project and all she contributed.

I appreciate all my coaches for their willingness to contribute their heartwarming Surrendering Stories to this project and their willingness to participate in the challenging editing process.

I'm thankful to Stefanie Herron for her passion for The Six Intimacy Skills™ and her offer to copyedit this manuscript.

I'm grateful for Thomas Elder's talented artistic design making my vision for the cover come to life.

I'm especially grateful for the loyal, passionate Kathy Murray for providing support and encouragement. I am a very lucky author to be surrounded by such a dedicated team.

One Last Thing…

If you enjoyed this book or found it useful, I'd be grateful if you'd post a review on Amazon.com. Your support really does make a difference, and I read every single review personally so I can get your feedback and make this book better.

If you'd like to leave a review, all you have to is to is go to the link on the book page on Amazon here:

Surrendered Wives Empowered Women Amazon

Thanks!

Laura

Other books by *New York Times* bestselling author Laura Doyle:

First, Kill All the Marriage Counselors: Modern Day Secrets to Being Desired, Cherished and Adored for Life

U.S	ITALY	MEXICO
U.K	NETHERLANDS	AUSTRALIA
GERMANY	JAPAN	INDIA
FRANCE	BRAZIL	
SPAIN	CANADA	

The Surrendered Wife: A Practical Guide to Intimacy, Passion and Peace with a Man

U.S	ITALY	MEXICO
U.K	NETHERLANDS	AUSTRALIA
GERMANY	JAPAN	INDIA
FRANCE	BRAZIL	
SPAIN	CANADA	

The Surrendered Single: A Practical Guide to Attracting and Marrying the Man Who's Right for You

U.S.	ITALY	MEXICO
U.K	NETHERLANDS	AUSTRALIA
GERMANY	JAPAN	INDIA
FRANCE	BRAZIL	
SPAIN	CANADA	

Things Will Get as Good as You Can Stand (When You Realize that it's Better to Receive than to Give)

U.S.	ITALY	MEXICO
U.K.	NETHERLANDS	AUSTRALIA
GERMANY	JAPAN	INDIA
FRANCE	BRAZIL	
SPAIN	CANADA	

La Esposa Entregada: Una Novedosa Estrategia para Alcanzar La Intimidad, La Pasión y La Armonía con Tu Esposo

U.S.	ITALY	MEXICO
U.K.	NETHERLANDS	AUSTRALIA
GERMANY	JAPAN	INDIA
FRANCE	BRAZIL	
SPAIN	CANADA	

About Laura Doyle

Laura Doyle is *The New York Times* best-selling author of *The Surrendered Wife, The Surrendered Single, Things Will Get As Good As You Can Stand (...When You Learn that It Is Better to Receive than to Give)*, and *First, Kill All the Marriage Counselors.*

Her books have been translated into seventeen languages and published in twenty-eight countries. Over 150,000 women credit her with not only saving their relationships but also showing them how to become desired, cherished, and adored for life.

She is the founder of Laura Doyle Connect, an international relationship coaching company that teaches women the Intimacy Skills they need to have passionate, peaceful relationships.

Laura has appeared on *CBS Evening News, Dateline NBC, The Today Show, Good Morning America,* and *The View.* She's been written about in *The Wall Street Journal, The New York Times, The Telegraph,* and *The New Yorker.*

Laura lives in Newport Beach, California, with her hilarious husband, John Doyle, who has been dressing himself since before she was born. They have been married for twenty-six years.